Diary
of a
Pissed-Off
Flight Attendant

Sydney Pearl

Diary of a Pissed-Off Flight Attendant
© Sydney Pearl, 2014

Edited by Full Sail Editing

ISBN-10: 099108232X

ISBN-13: 978-0-9910823-2-2

Contents

Author's Note

The characters and the events in this book are real. This is a nonfiction book loosely based on my experiences thus far in the airline industry. Because I am still currently an active flight attendant, I have had to use pseudonyms to protect the privacy of a few individuals and to cover my own ass. I have also taken certain storytelling liberties, particularly having to do with the section dedicated to my fellow crewmembers. I hope you take as much pleasure in reading my book as I did in writing it.

The following is dedicated to you, my dear passengers.

Chapter 1

Dear Diary,

This is my office, Motherf***ers!!

When you step from the jet bridge onto the airplane, you are entering my office. That tiny space I am standing in is the galley (also my office). The aisle you walk down to find your seat is my office too. The disgusting lavatories some of you seem to find so amusing? Also my office.

On an airplane, everything is compact by design. All the better to see you, my dear passengers, and all that you do in my domain.

Flight attendants always have eyes on you—whether it's a direct stare when you've really pissed one of us off, or a quick glance out of the corner of an eye—we are watching you.

When I fly with you, part of my job is spent sitting while we land, take off or ride out the turbulence. I also enjoy long breaks to eat, read and write. For the last year, my in-flight writing project has been this diary. Traditionally, flight attendants keep their thoughts about you to themselves, or talk about you behind your backs, but I think it's about time one of us shared a few observations with you.

THE WAY PEOPLE DRESS DRIVES ME CRAZY!

I take fashion very seriously. As the lead flight attendant, and fashionista, I rate your attire on a scale of one to ten when you board one of my flights. Unfortunately, I give more of you thumbs down than up. When a group of women flies with me and only one stands out because of her fabulous outfit, I compliment her . . . and only her. Then, I look away and I would whistle through the uncomfortable silence if I could because I refuse to give compliments where they aren't due.

I do not apologize if this offends you. You should apologize to me for wearing something so offensive in my place of business. If one of your friends told you that your outfit was cute, she lied. I want to ask some of you if you even own a mirror, but I don't.

I love southern California peeps, but there is a reason that so many serial killers come from the west coast—you people are crazy, ridiculous, self-serving, and needy. I have to hand it to you though; you do have the best bodies in North America. That doesn't mean we want to see them.

Recently, on a flight from Burbank to Las Vegas, a young woman boarded my flight wearing skin-tight boy shorts (with her butt cheeks peeking out), a tiny tank top, and tennis shoes. Read that again so you can let the image sink in. I'll wait. Okay? Now that you have the visual . . . yes, she was hot, but seriously, who dresses like that to travel?

Flights from Burbank to Las Vegas are usually packed with Botox-filled celebrities, people who want to be celebrities, or girls going to "work" (if you catch my drift). Maybe Miss Boy Shorts hoped someone would offer her a part in a movie. In California, people will do anything to be on the big screen.

Back in the day, people took pride in their appearances. Traveling was an event, an occasion. Now, it's like a free-for-all to be as skanky as possible. Some of you go another route, and put together looks that say "sleepover at an insane asylum". My first bit of advice? Get your s*** together, people! You don't have to be a fashion model, but at least wear clothes that fit, that are clean, and that aren't more suited to a costume party at Hugh Hefner's house.

LET US ENTERTAIN YOU . . . NOT!

When you know you are going to be traveling, you should come fully prepared with materials for your own entertainment. As flight attendants, we love our favorite "trash" (gossip) magazines and covet our treasures. They are wonderful treats to discover while we are cleaning up after you deplane. We look at them like rewards for doing the dirty job of cleaning up after you. So no. We won't lend them to you.

As I told you before, the galley is my office; that means you do not help yourself to my stash of magazines. If I find you reading my magazine, I will snatch it away and then politely ask, "Can I help you with something?", and watch you stutter and squirm because you were caught red-handed. And I will enjoy every minute of it. Now go back to your seat!

In this day and age, you are permitted to watch your small portable electronic device and you are free to listen to your music from the time you board the flight until you deplane. So, please do that and stop asking us if we are going to sing for you or tell you jokes. If you want to hear singing, plug in your headphones and if you want to hear jokes, go to the nearest Red Box and get yourself a comedy DVD for the road.

Recently, I was working an early morning flight from Chicago to Orlando when this lady boarded acting giddy and excited as if this was her first time flying.

"Good morning and welcome aboard," I said.

"Good morning to you too! Is this a singing flight?" she replied, rather loudly.

Confused, I asked, "What is a singing flight?"

"A flight where you sing us songs!" she explained.

"Ma'am, we are not at Disney yet, but we will be there shortly," I said, in a joking way although I was serious.

"You don't have to be so mean. I just wanted to hear a song," she said, grumbling under her breath and giving me the stink eye.

Excuse me? How am I being mean because you lack joy in your life at 5:00 AM? I'm sorry this is not the "happiest place on earth". Feel free to entertain yourself or go and bother your neighbors. Just don't bother me.

WHERE IS OUR FOOD?

When you see us at the airport, you may notice that we have at least three bags. We have a roller bag, a smaller bag for our manual and toiletries, and then we have another bag that resembles a food cooler (because it is one). We bring our food to work for the following reasons:

1. Our airline doesn't provide our food and we have to fend for ourselves, just like you do.
2. Most of us won't eat what we serve you because it's not healthy and it is full of preservatives.
3. We don't have time between flights to grab food.
4. We're very familiar with airports and what food they have to offer and, sadly, many airports have horrible food options.

Many times our meals can be quite decadent because they come from our homes and we make them special to treat ourselves after dealing with all of you. We do not appreciate it when we finally get a chance to enjoy our delicious home-cooked meal and you take the opportunity (as you wait for the lavatory) to comment on our food. These are the most common asides:

"Wow! That sure looks good."

"That's not fair! Did you bring enough for us?"

"Boy, I wish I could have a bite."

What I wish I could say the next time this happens:

"Of course it looks good! I made it."

"No, I didn't bring enough for you. Do you have an extra vacation for me?"

"Hell no! You cannot have a bite! Are you serious?"

Once, I left a bag of chips sitting on the galley counter

when I went to pick up trash in the cabin. When I came back, I discovered a guy (it's always some nasty man), had picked up my chips and was about to dig his hand into the bag.

"What the hell are you doing?" I asked him in my most authoritative tone.

Mr. Chip Grabber dropped the bag and his face turned red. "I was just looking at the ingredients."

Ingredients my ass! "Get out of my galley and go sit down!"

After that, he averted his eyes every time he saw me walking up and down the aisle. I sure taught him a lesson he won't forget about stealing other people's food!

In my office, we don't pass out food; however, we do pass out snacks on every flight. Notice I said we pass out snacks. If you're confused, let me clear this up for you . . . don't help yourself to our snacks! You could have just been in one of the disgusting restrooms, or digging in your nose, and you have the audacity to stick your hand in my serving basket to help yourself? If this was a help yourself situation, it would have been noted in your flight information and serving snacks would not be in my job description. If I'm taking too long for you because you are about to faint from hunger, let me remind you that every airport has vending machines, convenience stores, and multiple restaurants selling overpriced food. You—just like everyone else on the plane—could have stopped and picked yourself up a little something to tide you over. Plan, just like flight attendants and your more savvy travelers do, so that you don't have to lust after our lunch bags or get too cozy with the snack basket. Just a friendly reminder for next time.

Don't be surprised, if you ask a flight attendant, "Where's my food?" and she replies, "In the airport!" and then continues eating her meal, reading her book, and ignoring your unprepared ass.

ETIQUETTE ANYONE?

One afternoon, before doing my service, I heated up my food anticipating the lovely, hot meal I planned to enjoy undisturbed. After picking up your trash, I was finally ready to dig into my lunch. I got comfortable on my jumpseat, which is nicely placed next to the disgusting lavatory (yes, we have to smell you while we're eating our meals). I had my food on a tray, a bottle of water, and my magazine. Ah, lovely. I had just taken a bite when I heard someone exiting the restroom. When I didn't hear the person walk away, I looked around and saw a young woman doing the "downward dog" in my tiny galley.

"Excuse me, Miss, but you need to take your downward dog somewhere else. It's too small back here for yoga, and I am trying to eat," I told her.

"I'm sorry. I just needed to stretch. My legs are so sore," she said from her still upside down position, not budging.

I didn't really give a damn, but I kept my tone pleasant anyway. "I understand; however, the flight is only two hours long."

"I know, but when I fly I get really tight." She continued

to stretch.

"Have you considered a different mode of transportation?" Like, not on my airplane.

"No." She finally straightened her yoga-bending self out.

"You might want to check into that; however, now I need you to leave my galley please."

Miss Yoga looked at me, said "namaste" and left the galley.

Whatever, I thought.

I know. Sometimes flights are long and occasionally you need to stretch. Hey, I get it; however, doing yoga on an airplane is never acceptable. Let me put it in perspective for you. These days, the majority of you probably aren't fortunate enough to have your own office, but a few of you may have cubicles. Your cubicle has more square footage than my entire galley. I don't have a lovely break room or a lunchroom to escape to like you do. How would you feel if I came by your office to visit and then, while you were engrossed in your work or taking a well-earned break, I casually bent over and did a downward dog or pigeon pose? Would you feel a bit violated? Yeah, that's what I thought.

HEY, YOU . . . BUSINESS PASSENGER SITTING IN THE FRONT ROW . . .

I see you're absorbed in your book and have no idea what's going on around you. But I watched you stick your finger in your nose and then insert that same finger in your mouth. How did it taste? Was it salty? Sweet? As disgusting as it looked? When you picked your nose the second time, looked at it, and then flicked it away, you were lucky it didn't end up on my shoe or we would have had a serious problem. As it is, I'm just grossed out by you.

If you are fortunate enough to have an entire row to yourself, feel free to sleep on your side or on your stomach. I don't appreciate walking down the aisle and coming across you, asleep on your back with your legs hanging open and your crotch on full display. Gross! If you are snoring too (and you usually are), I am thoroughly disgusted with you. Don't hang your legs over the seat into the aisle either. Yes, you've paid for a seat, but you're on borrowed time here, so show a little respect or we might not allow you to come back again.

Ever hear the phrase, "Do unto others as you would have them do unto you"? This goes double when you're visiting someone else's place of business.

Remember when I told you that we're always watching you? My jumpseat has the best view in the house. If you know you drool while sleeping, please don't sit in the front row because we'll laugh at you. Do not sit in the front row if you sleep with your mouth hanging open either because, if I am bored, I might just play a game to see if I can land a peanut in your gaping mouth. We flight attendants have to entertain ourselves too you know!

Bare Feet on the Armrests? Are you Serious?

It saddens me that I have to include this as a topic of discussion, but alas, I do. Last week, while working a flight from

Philadelphia to Fort Lauderdale, I was walking through the cabin doing the normal trash routine when I walked by a display that made me double back because I wasn't sure if my eyes were playing tricks on me. A dad sat with his two teenage daughters. Normal so far. But the girl sitting by the window had her shoes off. One of her nasty feet was on top of the armrest and the other sat on the tray table.

I almost choked at the trashiness of the situation, but managed to find my voice. "Excuse me, but you need to remove your feet from that armrest and that tray table, young lady."

Her eyes opened wide and she looked at her dad, who now sported a goofy look on his face.

"I am so sorry, Miss. Amber, get your feet down and put your shoes back on," the dad told his disgusting daughter.

While I am glad he didn't argue, he was still an ass because he'd been aware of his daughter's misconduct and hadn't even thought of correcting her until I came by. You have to wonder what goes on when people like this are at home if they act this way in public.

Other people occupy your seat when you leave. The airplane is not fully cleaned until the end of the night, so the next set of passengers will unsuspectingly be subjected to your filthy manners.

BODY PARTS IN THE AISLE?

I understand you may be 6'8" and you possess clodhoppers for feet, but please be respectful and keep those suckers out of my way. Kindly place your luggage in the overhead bin so that the space you paid for in front of you is available for your feet. You did not pay for the aisle I have to work in; therefore, I should not have to ask you multiple times to move your feet out of my way. After three times, I get ugly and you are liable to be injured.

Once, I was working in the back portion of the plane on a Wednesday-night flight from Houston to Dallas. It was what we call a "business flight" (not in reference to seat class, but to particular city codes and times of the day. Early morning flights between 5:00 AM and 9:00 AM that are around one to one and a half hours or less are usually flights full of men and women going to business meetings for the day. Around 3:00 PM to 7:00 PM, this same group of people returns for their flights home). Maybe it's because of the stress caused by closing deals, losing deals, or just because you're heading home to deal with your significant other, you guys can get damned stupid with your constant ordering of spirits at 30,000 feet. On this particular forty-minute flight, I was busting my ass serving up cocktails and, as I was running up and down the aisle delivering drinks, I had to ask this guy to move his feet from the aisle.

The first time I said, "Please remove your feet from the aisle because someone may trip."

The next time I came by, his foot was in the aisle again.

"Sir, please move your feet," I said.

The third time I found his feet in the aisle, I said, "Look, I'm working here and I'm tired of asking you to move your feet."

I thought that would do it, but when it didn't, I took matters into my own hands. I took off my service flats and put back on my 3 1/2" heels. As I was walking down the aisle, I "accidentally" stepped on Mr. Foot-in-the-Aisle's foot and dug my heel in. He screamed his ass off, but guess what? We did not have another conversation about him moving his feet from the aisle again.

You might think that was mean, but I am sure my fellow flight attendants would agree when I say tough shit.

WHY DO PEOPLE LOVE TO CONGREGATE IN THE GALLEY?

Due to the events of 9/11, several new security measures were put into place. Number one being that you cannot congregate for any reason near the cockpit. If you happen to be on an aircraft where the forward lavatory is near the cockpit, you can't stand, stretch, or talk near the cockpit/forward lavatory. You have to remain in your seat until the lavatory is available.

Usually, when the seat belt sign goes off, I make a P.A. (public announcement) that goes a little something like this: "Ladies and gentlemen, the seat belt sign has been turned off. You are now free to use the lavatories onboard. We have two lavatories onboard this aircraft—one in the front and one in the rear. However, due to federal regulations, you may not form a line in the forward part of the aircraft. If you see this "X" sign (I point to the ceiling sign to illustrate), that means the lavatory is occupied. You must remain in your seat until it is available or you are free to use the lavatory in the back of the plane."

That seems straightforward, doesn't it? Then why, after twelve years, do we still have to remind some of you?

"I am sorry, Ma'am, but the lavatory is occupied. You're going to have to go back to your seat and wait or you are more than welcome to use the lavatory in the back." I know you see me sitting on the forward jumpseat, but do I really look like a bathroom monitor to you?

"Well, there is a line back there." You frown as if lines are not something we all encounter every day.

"I am sorry about that, but you still cannot stand in the front portion of the aircraft."

Your response? You move two rows back down the aisle and stand there.

"Ma'am, you cannot stand in the front of the aircraft . . . period," I tell you.

We both hear the toilet flush and, giving me a superior look, you march back up to the front . . . and stand.

"Ma'am, I am not going to tell you a third time. Just because they flushed does not mean they are ready to come out."

You test me for another second, staying right where you are, then slowly walk away as you realize they are not coming out after all.

I am not going to reveal what steps would have been taken next if I had to keep talking to you, but let's just say it would involve a call to the captain and a possible meeting with authorities at your next stop. Yes! This rule is that serious!

The only exception to the "no standing by the cockpit" rule is when little kids or the elderly are involved. I am not a babysitter, so if a parent cannot fit in the lavatory with their kid, I will allow them to wait outside. Same with the elders. I hope they have someone to assist them, as I am not a nurse either and will not help them with their Depends.

One day, when I was working a flight from Boston to Tampa, a passenger in a wheelchair came onboard. I was informed by the operations agent that Betty could barely walk and that she did not have anyone traveling with her. I was concerned about getting her back and forth to the lavatory as she also did not have a cane. The agent told me not to worry, that Betty had assured him that she was wearing her Depends and that it would last her the entire flight. About half way into the flight, Betty must have had too many beverages because she told me that she needed to go to the restroom. After getting her into the lavatory, I went back to the galley and continued reading my book. Soon after, the lavatory door banged open and there was Betty, sitting on the toilet with her "diaper" around her ankles for the entire world to see.

"Miss, I could use some help here," she said, as if that wasn't totally obvious.

I was so shocked that I froze in place for a few seconds, just staring at her with my mouth hanging open. When I was able to talk, I asked her just what kind of help she needed.

She said that she needed me to change her Depends. *Oh, hell no*, I thought. I called the other two flight attendants and they both gleefully declined to help her. I explained to Betty that I had hepatitis and that she did not want me near her and her privates. I apologized and told her that she would just have to pull her Depends back up and sit tight for the duration of the flight.

While you can stand in the back to wait for the restroom, on some of our planes the restroom is located in the galley. If I'm eating, you are hovering over me. If we hit clear air turbulence (turbulence is the cause of the majority of injuries onboard an airplane), and you are not holding on to something, and I am sitting on my beloved jumpseat, you will fall on me, most likely causing us both harm. If I am working, you are in my way. I shouldn't have to navigate around you in my own damned office!

Don't loiter. Use the restroom and keep it moving please! If you see flight attendants engrossed in conversation, you may not chime in because we will either ignore you or give you the look of death. If you are unattractive, you had better high tail it back to your seat. The same goes for you Mr. Overly Arrogant. Keep your ass moving too. Unless you truly are super cool and we might actually find you interesting, just do us all a big favor, and stay out of our space please.

CROP DUSTING IS A POWERFUL TOOL IN A FLIGHT ATTENDANT'S BAG OF TRICKS

Are you familiar with this term? No, silly, we do not actually crop dust cornfields. Crop dusting has a completely different meaning among flight attendants when we pass gas as we're walking down the aisle. We really get a sick pleasure from letting one fly and looking back to see who is blamed. You'll never know it was us because we are too quick, and though the cloud lingers, we'll have long since disappeared.

This fly-by technique also works if you have pissed us off in some way. Wondering why the flight attendant you talked back to is suddenly lingering around your seat? You smell that? I just ate quinoa and broccoli, so it's extra foul today. I sincerely apologize for that. Not.

Have a great day!

Chapter 2

Bird Strikes Back

For the first several years of my life, I lived with my paternal grandparents, George and Audrey, and my aunt, Shirl. I was the apple of my grandparent's eyes and I relished their love and affection. My grandmother did not work because my aunt Shirl was mentally disabled and required 24/7 care. My grandfather worked at the General Motors plant.

I loved when his payday rolled around and I could collect my allowance. Every two weeks, I looked forward to going to K-Mart to peruse the latest in fashions by Kathy Ireland. We did not have a lot of money, so I checked out what the wealthy kids were wearing at school and then would get something similar from K-Mart or Payless.

Although I loved my bi-weekly shopping excursions, nothing compared to my love for school. I LOVED school and I looked forward to going every day until I got to the 5th grade. I was always an extremely popular kid. I was smart and I never had a shortage of friends.

Later in life, I realized that my popularity had a lot less to do with my looks and intelligence than I had thought back then. I was what we now know as a "token" (thanks South

Park). Yep, I was the token black chick among all of my white classmates, and got along with all of them. But at the bus stop, among the black kids, was a whole other story. The black kids constantly picked on me and teased me because of my smart mouth and because they said I "talked white". Apparently, speaking proper English is a no-no among some kids.

The black kid's favorite nickname for me was Bird. The teasing went on for weeks. I never responded to them and finally took my tears to my beloved grandmother. "Grandmom, those black kids keep making fun of me at the bus stop. They call me Bird and they say I talk white."

Grandmom smiled gently. "You are special. You have a graceful neck and a beautiful clavicle. You talk properly and you are smarter than all of them. They are jealous of you."

Huh? *What the hell is a clavicle*, I thought.

"Never mind those idiots. You just repeat after me, 'God made dirt and dirt don't hurt. Sticks and stones may break my bones, but words will never hurt me.' And you will be just fine." As always, Grandmom seemed so sure.

"Okay. If you say so," I said, trying to believe it the way she did.

When the next school day rolled around, I was feeling proud of myself and my profound intelligence, bathed in the wisdom of my grandmother. That is, I felt this way until the taunts started again. During the worst of it, I repeated my new mantras over and over, and when I refused to react to the bullying, the other kids pulled on my dry-ass jeri curl (for you white folks, that's a curly perm) and started making fun of my Kathy Ireland Collection outfit and my Nikes that were noticeably missing the swoosh.

I stood with clenched fists, but still did not respond. I was resilient and I was showing them!

"Hey, bird shit!" Maria, my main antagonist said, grinning in my face.

"My grandmother said I have a graceful neck and a beautiful clavicle, so there!" I'd wished Maria dead on a daily basis and wanted to stick my tongue out, but I satisfied myself with words alone.

"What the fuck is a clavicle?! Are you insulting my intelligence?" Her chin jutted out and her eyes narrowed.

I shrugged. "Well, you know what they say about the shoe fitting." I rolled my neck the way I'd seen my mother do a thousand times.

My triumph lasted only for the fleeting second it took Maria to smack me square in the face.

I cried and ran home. By this time, I had moved in with my mother Janice. Getting wind of my anti-fighting stance, even when someone smacked me in the face, she walked me to the bus stop the next day and went off on Maria. I love my mother, but she's ghetto and known for her perpetual scowl. She's hefty, not from genetics, but because she's lazy. You never know what color her hair is going to be, but it's always in a ponytail jutting from the side of her head. She's always chewing Double Bubble bubble gum. In other words, people run when they see Janice coming.

"I'm not going to let you ruin my reputation," she told me, never mind my own reputation or the state of my face.

To the bullies, she said, "You start something and she don't kick your asses, I will."

Trust me, you would rather run away than get your ass kicked by my mother. I hated Janice and wanted to die from embarrassment, but I also felt certain that Maria's bullying days were over.

Still, I spent that night practicing. My brothers and I loved WWE and Punch Out on Nintendo. We also had a pair of boxing gloves and I begged them to teach me some fighting moves. We had a mini boot camp and by the next morning I was all pumped up and I even ate a little oatmeal for courage. I strutted to the bus stop ready to fight, with my chest puffed out. All those good feelings lasted until Maria "accidentally" tripped me.

I began breathing hard and I started to cry again, but this time I didn't feel sad. I was mad as a mother f***er!

Maria started getting all soul sister on me, up in my face and pointing her finger.

"Bitch, if you are so tough, meet me in the church parking lot after school," I said (in the extremely proper manner she'd teased me about).

Why the church parking lot? I needed Jesus or a miracle to save my ass!

All the other kids started getting excited at the prospect of a fight, but I wanted to piss my pants at the thought of actually having to go through with it.

Throughout the day, I was sweating and could not eat. I was glad I'd had the oatmeal for breakfast. Most days seemed to drag by minute by minute, but this one flew by quickly, too quickly, until I found myself surrounded by kids from school and Maria, baiting me as if I was a black bear, in the Mount Olive Baptist Church parking lot.

As she circled, I just stood there, getting angrier and angrier by the second. She said something about my mother and that was the tipping point because nobody can talk about my mother except me. I blacked out and went into a blind rage. All I remember is people pulling me off of Maria while she cried and said she was sorry.

From that day forward, I carried a major chip on my shoulder, and kept a beast within on a leash. I became popular with the black kids and, after a few more fights, I started hanging with the wrong crowd. I began to retaliate against Janice and ran away from home. My aunt Melanie started taking me in so I would have a stable home environment. After a lot of back and forth, my mother finally saw the potential in me and, wanting me to have better opportunities in life than she could provide, she had a long talk with my aunt Melanie. At the age of twelve, I was adopted by my aunt Melanie and my uncle James and left my five younger siblings to go live in the big state of Texas.

Though I lived in a few places, and had different examples of how to parent, I was always raised to be a proper girl with the best of manners. Maybe that's why I have trouble understanding the way some of you act on airplanes when it comes to your kids.

Chapter 3

Dear Diary,

Why do they think our multimillion-dollar jet is a daycare center?

I am not a parent and I do not profess to know how hard or easy it really is; however, I do know that when the day comes for me to be a parent, I will not be lazy. I know you are probably saying, "You will eat those words," but I know that I won't.

You don't know me, but I am very active and fit, and I lead by example. I will make sure my children are not only responsible and productive members of society, but that they also look and dress the part, unlike the kid in the next story.

I was working an early morning flight with one eye open and one eye closed. I was very tired and sleepily going through the motions when on came a family that woke me up a little. While the parents were dressed in decent clothes, the kids (who were awake and walking) were still in their pajamas.

"Can you please help us find our seats?" the dad asked.

"Sure, let me direct you to our bunk bed section in the back of the plane," I said, smirking.

I don't care how early it is, when you fly you are going to

end up somewhere in the world other than your own bed. It's uncouth for your kids to arrive at your destination in their pajamas. And, as a parent, you are already setting the precedent that it is okay to wear pajamas in public. When your kids are older, they will think this is the norm (it is not!). I understand that Suzy might be cranky in the morning and that you did not want to wake her. Be proactive, and dress her the night before. Let her sleep in her dress or wake her ass up in the morning and make her deal with it! Who is the adult around here?

And while you're at it, please do something with your own appearance. Showing up at the airport wearing rollers, silk bonnets, and shower caps is never a "do". It will always be an emphatic "don't". How could you show your face in public looking like that? I am sick and tired of women showing up with multiple kids, multiple gadgets, multiple strollers, multiple bags, and multiple shit with no man or nanny to assist them. I am busy doing my job, so that means I do not have the time to hold Tanner while you rally Steven, Ashley, and Jennifer because they are running amuck. I did not impregnate you and I am not the damned help. So watch yourself, and save the attitude because you should have thought about all of this before deciding to have the little weasels. I can say this, and be mean, because I do encounter women who seem to handle this very situation with gusto and finesse, unlike the others who can't seem to get a handle on life.

Why do they travel with sick Children?

During the cold and flu season, flight attendants carry around a pharmacy in our luggage because we do not want to get sick. We cannot work if we are sick. We hate it when you come onboard our flight with your dirty kids and their runny noses, smelly diapers, and swollen eyes. You wonder why they are crying? They are crying because they are sick and know that they are disgusting. They are tired and you have forced them to be here when they would rather be at home in their cribs. Hell, I want them to be home in their cribs too.

Please do not ask me to hold your dirty-ass child while you go to the restroom, collapse your five-fold stroller, or for any reason, because I will politely decline. Let's look at this picture: I am in my nicely pressed and starched uniform, and you are dressed in mom jeans and a t-shirt, holding your baby who is wearing a stained onesie. If you have caught me in a vulnerable moment, I may agree to hold Junior (at arm's length, as far away from me as possible). When I do, don't give me that disgusted look as if to say, "Really?", because I will give you an equally "Really?" look and go a step further and put my nose in the air to let you know that this whole situation is disgusting and far beneath me.

Let me give you a friendly suggestion. Save some extra money and hire someone to travel with you or take your mother on a "vacation". We would appreciate any help you bring.

TRAVELING ISN'T PLAYTIME

I am certain that I left the jungle gym and monkey bars at my elementary school playground. I am also certain that the multimillion-dollar jet I proudly work on is not your backyard swing set. So why don't you know this? Why is your child running around and jumping from seat to seat? Are you confused or have you bumped your head and you don't know where you are? Let me enlighten you.

You are on a jet that is so expensive that you couldn't afford to replace the window shade, so I suggest that you control your brat and that he stops pulling on the damned shade before he breaks one.

I know that is not Play-Doh I spy. Are you kidding me? You may allow whatever you want in your home or in your own car—which probably smells like old McDonald's french fries—but, around here, Play-Doh is a no-no! What makes you think it is okay for little Joey to mold Play-Doh into the carpet or on the tray table? You do know that when you deplane, there will be countless others sitting in this same seat, right? Oh, you don't care? How about if my lovely airline hits your ass with a bill? Would you care then? I thought so.

Stop taking advantage of our kindness. I know you thought that just because you sat in the front row and have all that extra legroom, that Cicely can use this space as her play area. Well, she can't, not while the seat belt sign is on and certainly not without parental supervision.

I suggest that you keep hold of your child because if they wander into my aisle when I'm doing my cabin service, you and I are going to have a chat and then Cicely will not be playing the rest of the flight.

TRAY TABLES ARE NOT FOR ASSES

I just know that's not a baby's naked ass on the tray table of my multimillion-dollar jet is it? Are you really changing his diaper on the tray table?

On any aircraft, there is at least one changing table located in the bathroom (not in your seat!). I don't care if you have been waiting forever to use the restroom. Those baby-changing tables are expensive and were installed for your benefit.

Perhaps more importantly, did you see that pedophile sitting across the aisle checking out your baby's ass? Get a clue people; they are everywhere!

If I find another Goldfish cracker, I will scream bloody murder. I HATE finding Goldfish crackers with their cheddar smells. They are always on the floor, between the seats, in the seat-back pockets or sometimes soggily sitting on a tray table because even your child is fed up with the disgusting crackers. If you allow your children to eat these Goldfish crackers or any other snack (including Cheerios, peanuts, or pretzels) off the tray, I will remind you that although you are on a state-of-the-art jet, it's only thoroughly cleaned once a day . . . at the end of the day. So when you come on midday, countless things have been on your tray table—naked-ass baby bottoms, drool from someone sleeping, dirty feet, and drinks that have been spilled. That table has not been cleaned with a disinfectant, only wiped off with a napkin and refolded back to its original position awaiting the next atrocity.

DON'T THEY REALIZE THEIR CHILD'S BEHAVIOR PROBLEMS AFFECT EVERYONE AROUND THEM?

I know you are a good parent and that you feel as if you need the approval of everyone around you, but guess what? We don't give a shit. The only thing we care about is that you make sure your kids keep their asses in their seats and that they are quiet. Flight attendants will give crying babies a pass because there's nothing you can do about that. However, I still love it when other passengers ring their call button over a crying baby.

"Miss, is there anything you can do about that noise?" the passenger asks, tossing an angry glare toward the offending infant.

"I am sorry. What noise?" Of course, I know what noise.

"That crying baby!"

"Oh, you mean the crying baby who can't tell me what's wrong so I can stop its crying? What do you suggest I do . . . tell the parents?"

I can't make your babies stop crying and I never say anything to parents in this situation, but if your child is old enough to talk, that's another issue altogether.

I often find myself playing the role of unpaid nanny and it chaps my hide. I hate when you, the supposed adult, can't control your child and then you look to me for help. Again, I don't have any kids, but I will show you how it's done. I will get eye level with your little brat and give them "the look". As a child, when I would misbehave, my mother would get in my face and just stare at me without blinking. She would purse her lips, raise her eyebrows and silently look at me for a few seconds. You can give people the "look" when trying to correct someone's behavior or if someone says or does something too silly for words. If done correctly, the "look" will remedy most situations. I will look your child in the eye and tell them that they must be in their seat with their seat belt fastened unless they want to come with me. In most cases, the child immediately straightens up for fear of going with someone with some authority. Problem solved.

Next time your child is acting up on a plane, I suggest you take their little asses into the restroom and show them who's boss.

THIS ISN'T STORYTIME

Reading out loud is fine at home, but not in public (unless you are in a library, and even then, this rude behavior is confined to story hour). Maybe you don't know the rules of reading in public. One is to read to yourself, quietly (that means to read with your mind not your mouth).

When you take it upon yourself to prove to the world that you are a good parent because you are reading to your child aloud, all you are doing is pissing people off. Nobody cares how articulate you are or about the fact that you can read. Nobody wants to hear the tales of Dr. Seuss. How would you feel if the man across from you started reading aloud from his *Maxim* magazine, or if the lady in front of you started reading her *Fifty Shades of Grey* novel? Are you rolling your eyes? Good, because we are too!

Breast-feeding should be a private affair

I understand how important breast-feeding is, and know this is going to piss some of you off, but is it too much to ask you not to do it in my office? It is quite acceptable if you have a cover up and I strongly and silently suggest that you do just that and please go a step further and sit by the window. Nobody, and I mean nobody, except the perverts we carry daily (and no, they do not wear signs on their foreheads), wants to see your huge, veiny, discolored boobs. I get that breast-feeding is natural, but so is taking a dump; however, I will politely close the door so my facial expressions and grunts don't offend you.

Years ago, I was working a flight from Oakland to Portland. I have to pause here and admit that I am not a fan of "granola" people. You know, Birkenstocks, any type of dread locks (especially on white people), hairy women who think mustaches are acceptable, and "natural" body odor. I have to point this out because between these two cities we get many passengers who fit this description. Anyway, on this particular flight, I could smell there would be trouble when a woman came onboard and I had to curl my lip and hold my breath as she passed by, unable to give her a fake smile. She sported blond, dirty dread locks, looked, smelled all-natural, and carried a boy who should have been walking since he looked about five-years old.

Later, as I was taking drink orders, I noticed that she was seated in the last part of my section. When I got to her, not only was she seated in an aisle seat, but she was breast-feeding her son without a cover-up in sight.

"Ma'am, can I get you something to drink?" I said, trying not to breathe through my nose or look at her boob.

"I would like a Coke," Rainbow said (granola people always have earthy names).

Wow, a Coke while breast-feeding, I thought. Okay. "Sure ma'am, I'll be right back," I said.

"I want a Coke too," the "baby" said, after the nipple popped out of his mouth.

WTF?! I was dumbfounded and stood as if rooted to the spot for a few seconds trying to comprehend what had just happened.

After sharing this story with my fellow crewmembers and then the obligatory walk down the aisle from said crewmembers to identify the culprit, I brought Rainbow her Coke and the baby his Coke in a sippy cup. After all these years, I am still shaking my head.

Chapter 4

A Fashionista is Born

Like many young girls, when dreaming of a career as a flight attendant, I only saw the romantic image and no downside to the job at all. Unlike other young girls, I had my very own role model, my aunt Claire, a flight attendant for Sun Airways during the 80's. I worshipped her and was enthralled from our first meeting. I loved trying on her clothes and parading around her house on a makeshift runway. She deserves full credit for forming me into the fashionista I am today.

Aunt Claire had every beauty product one could ever need, save for self-tanner. She always had the latest *Vogue* or *Cosmopolitan* magazines too. I sifted through them all, and wished I could afford anything by a high-end designer.

She enjoyed a lot of time off. When she visited, I would sit around and absorb her stories about the exotic-sounding places she visited and the adventures she had on overnight trips, and about the celebrities she met. Her career sounded like so much fun!

I had an even temperament and got along well with people (after a rough patch as a younger child). I'd be a natural at her job, I remember thinking. I also recall being a well-behaved and sweet child even at a young age. I imagined that I had come into this world peacefully. But my mother had a totally different account, I learned later in life.

In early ultrasound shots, I peacefully rested inside my mother and appeared serene, without a care in the world. Then, I was yanked out of my reverie and all hell broke loose.

I was born in Michigan during a full moon and came out screaming and complaining, with my tiny face all scrunched up as if I was angry as hell. I was a very good child. I rarely got spanked. I was taught good manners and I was always smiling. I was also a mischievous little thing. I was smart and possessed a smart-ass mouth.

Laughing was something I did often, much to the chagrin of my grandparents. Anything would set me off into hysterics—a random fart, somebody belching, somebody tripping over their own two feet. Pretty much anything would send me into a fit that would last way past being funny. To this day, I still crack up over other people's mishaps.

Chapter 5

Dear Diary,

Do they check their brains along with their luggage?

We are well aware that sometimes traveling can be stressful. On our personal days off, we travel as regular passengers too, and we know that any number of things can cause a disruption. However, please keep in mind that there are TV monitors all over the terminals showing the gate and departure time of your flight, giving you no reason to harass every airline employee you encounter to ask about your flight. The TV monitors also display whether your flight is on time or delayed. With the invention of smart phones there are also quite a few apps you can download that will also give you this information. Did you know that you can type in your flight information on the Flight Tracker app and it will give you the time you are scheduled to land? Yes? Then why do you keep asking me all of your stupid questions?

WHAT TIME DO WE LAND?

Didn't you set up some type of transportation at your destination? Whether you are picking up a car, getting picked up from the airport, or you have a connecting flight, you should know what time you are scheduled to land!

Don't you have a watch? What about checking your phone's clock?

On a recent flight, I was not in the best of moods and it was for the best that I had as little contact with passengers as possible. Of course, that's when someone had to interrupt me with this innocuous question:

"What time do we land?"

"I don't know," I answered.

The passenger looked at me as if I was an idiot.

I looked at him the same way, then smiled my most fake smile and walked away.

Let me explain something to you. We make announcements at the beginning of the flight telling you exactly how long the flight is so you can calculate the flight time. Our pilots also make announcements telling you exactly how long the flight will be. You were busy talking on your cell phone? Oh well. Sounds like a personal problem to me.

Sometimes flight attendants genuinely do not know the time we are scheduled to land because we have so many flights that we work during the day and our only concern is what time we are going to reach our final destination. We do have what is called a trip sheet. A trip sheet provides us with our entire itinerary for each trip. We know what cities we are going to, what time we take off and land in each city, and how much time we have on the ground between each of our flights. Although I usually keep my trip sheet in my pocket, if you caught me in a bad mood, and I don't feel like pulling it out for you, you're out of luck. So there.

WHAT ARE WE FLYING OVER?

Our extensive and intensive training deals with emergencies and procedures onboard the aircraft and we do not concern ourselves with the geological areas we fly over. We are usually too busy running back and forth taking care of you and the few moments we have to ourselves are not spent caring about what we are flying over. We care about one thing: getting to our final destination of the day.

When I'm in the middle of the aircraft passing out drinks, unable to see anything but the whiteness of clouds, and you are sitting by the window looking down at whatever you are looking at, and you ask me, "What are we flying over?", I will probably respond with, "I don't know. Let me pull my Rand McNally out of my pocket and check." If I am in a really snarky mood and you ask me what we are flying over, I might say, "The sky."

The other day, we were flying from California to Kansas City and, as I was passing out drinks, I noticed a passenger who was reading our inflight magazine's article about Mount Rushmore. Every time I walked by him, he'd ask me innocuous questions until I started to get frustrated with the constant questions.

"Miss, what are we flying over?" he asked.

I looked at him with a straight face and said, "Mount Rushmore."

I am directionally and geographically challenged, but I

am not clueless. I give passengers these goofy responses to demonstrate just how much I don't care about what we're flying over. And since I have proven to you just how dumb I am, maybe you will stop asking me questions.

ARE WE THERE YET?

I want to meet the people who created the show, *Are We There Yet?* (and this tired and ridiculous question) and smack them. When someone asks me this stupid-ass question, my responses depend on what kind of mood I'm in. I usually reply, "Does it look like it?" or, "I don't know, are we?" or, "What do you think?"

I really don't like working in the summer or during the holidays, because we usually encounter less seasoned travelers and they just do not have a clue about how what to say and what not to say to the flight crew. I think in between their yearly trips, these people sit around thinking of lines they think we'll find funny. Little do they know, we have heard almost every line a million times and we don't find them funny anymore.

Last month, a family of five boarded my flight. I could tell from the goofy smile on the dad's face that he was dying for some attention from me. He told me that it was his daughter, Hailey's, birthday and then had the nerve to ask if we could sing her a song. I told him that it was too early in the morning and reminded him that we needed to be considerate of the other passengers. I wished Hailey a happy birthday and then turned my attention elsewhere. About thirty minutes into our six-hour flight, goofy dad needed a pillow and blanket. I explained that we did not have pillows and blankets onboard. Since we discontinued those disgusting things years ago I wondered how long it had been since he'd flown. I had a feeling he was going to be a constant pain in my ass so I tried my best to avoid him.

Later in the flight, I was sitting in my galley and saw him go into the lavatory.

When he came out, he paused. "Are we there yet?" He stood there with a silly smile on his face.

I just looked at him and said, "We will be, in about four more hours."

What I really wanted to say is this: "Look here, idiot, if we were there, you wouldn't be asking ME this question because guess what? We'd be there and you'd be gone."

Thanks jackass, this flight just got that much longer.

HOW DO YOU OPEN THE BATHROOM DOOR?

Even if you wear glasses, I will not forgive you for asking me this because I know most of you can read, if not words than the pictures near every handle on an airplane.

Let me hold your hand and point out a few things. The two most common doors found on an aircraft will either be the pull or push variety. With the pull variety, there is a silver handle you pull up or down (usually down) and then you enter. With the push variety, the door will be accordion style with the word "PUSH" in big letters somewhere on the door. You push and voila, the door folds in and you can enter.

Before you attempt to enter the onboard lavatory, please look to see if the sign near the door handle is green or red, or if it says vacant or occupied. Sorry for including you geniuses with the less fortunate, but some people just don't quite know what any of that stuff means. As a rule, in everyday life, green means "go" and red means "stop". Vacant means "empty" and occupied means "busy or not available". So the next time I am taking my union break on my jumpseat and reading my book, please don't bother me and ask, "Is this vacant?" because my response will be, "I don't know. Is it?" I am engrossed in my book and have no idea what the sign says, but you (you clever devil) are in a position to read your own damned sign.

Oh, and another thing about the bathroom . . . stop asking us, "How do you flush the toilet?"

Do you see that sign that says . . . FLUSH? If not, I sincerely suggest you go see an eye doctor.

JIGGLING THE BATHROOM DOOR

When you approach the door and notice that the sign says occupied, I can understand trying to turn the doorknob because sometimes the sign can be faulty. What I don't understand is, when you realize that the lavatory is occupied, why you still stand there and jiggle the door handle.

Why?! Jiggling the door handle is not going to make the person inside go any faster. All you are doing is pissing them off, annoying me while I am trying to read my book in peace, and proving to everyone watching you just how stupid you really are.

I had the pleasure of witnessing such an event where the man in the restroom opened the door with his pants around his legs, and yelled at the door-jiggling lady. She stood there looking as if she was on the verge of tears. When she walked away, I was laughing so hard that I almost peed my pants.

Lost Items

I lost my wallet. I lost my iPad. I lost my phone. I lost my purse. I lost my shoes. I lost my socks. On and on the lost item list goes. My luxury jet is NOT your home, so I do not understand why you get so comfortable that you unpack as if you are staying for the weekend.
If you are on a transatlantic flight, you are forgiven, but you domestic travelers need to be popped on the side of your heads.

According to the airline's F.A.R. (federal aviation regulation), no items may be placed in your seat-back pocket besides the items the airline has placed there. This usually includes the FAA mandated safety information card, an airsick bag, a magazine specific to the airline, and a menu detailing what food, drinks, snacks and goods are available for purchase onboard the aircraft. Notice, I did not say your wallet, iPad, cell phone, Kindle, purse, shoes, socks, hats, water bottles, coffee cups, kids' diapers, toys, or magazines. So if you have committed this offense and lost your belongings, you deserved to lose them. Thanks for the magazines, the cash (now I can buy dinner!), those brand new Gucci sunglasses (score!) and the new movies you brought but did not watch (yay!).

People do steal. This includes the people sitting next to you and your lovely flight attendants. Passengers with sense are used to people like you who lack sense, so as they deplane, sometimes they move slowly down the aisle and check each row of seats to see what has been left behind. Sometimes they turn things in to us, or tell us about an item that has been left, but sometimes they help themselves to your lost items. First come, first served.

If we become aware of items that have been left behind, we have to make a moral decision on whether we want to be a Good Samaritan while weighing how badly we really covet this particular item. Unfortunately for you, many times we decide that we could really use what you left behind. Unfortunately for us, sometimes we are busted. The majority of electronic devices are equipped with a tracking device, and there have been quite a few flight attendants and gate agents who have been fired for having passengers' items in their personal possession without any explanation.

In one of our west-coast cities, there was an agent who had been with the company for twenty years when, one day, an iPad was turned in to her. She did not turn it in to Lost and Found, but instead took it home. The smart passenger who'd lost it tracked it to her home and that was the end of the agent's twenty-year career.

Another time, a flight attendant in the south decided to take home a laptop that belonged to a federal agent . . . oops!

My beloved company has a zero tolerance policy for theft and dishonesty. That is why I don't ever keep electronic devices I find on an aircraft. I am going to plead the fifth on everything else. Hehehe.

While tidying (I do not clean) up the plane one day, I came across some worn socks (I am not joking). It is a good thing that I wear gloves or I would have puked. How could someone get off the plane without their socks? What in the hell happened? Because that person was so gross, their socks are now in the trash. I hope their feet are cold now.

The point is, stop undressing and tucking in. Keep your things intact and take all of your belongings with you when you deplane. But, hey, feel free to continue to leave the unopened bags of candy and chips behind because we're hungry.

CHECKING BAGS

Recently, airlines have changed their policies and are now starting to charge you for your excessive luggage. Jet fuel is more expensive now than ever before, so if you want to lug everything to the airport, including your kitchen sink, you will now have to pay for it.

Every airline has a limit as to how many bags you can bring onboard. Anything outside of the limitations will have to be checked and yes, you will be charged. It would be wise of you to know your airline's policy before trying to board our planes as each airline allows a different number of bags and has differing rules on what size bags are allowed in the cabin.

The airlines are out to make money, and the gate agents will be on your bags like fleas if they do not meet the guidelines. No, they do not have a quota to make and no, they do not get a bonus check for bags they check. They are simply doing their jobs and are rather tired of you bringing all of your crap onboard and then having the nerve to ask for assistance.

We only have so much bin space and we would really like to be able to accommodate everyone's luggage. I have better things to do than to check your bags, but when the bins are full, they are full and there is nothing we can do about it. No, I will not climb on the seats and rearrange other people's luggage. What do I look like, a damned monkey? There is no need to get an attitude with me because people have their coats in spaces that should be for bags; just put your bag on top of their coats, dirty wheels and all. Why? Because we constantly make announcements asking people to be courteous and to hold onto their jackets until the bin is full. We also warn them about the possibility of getting their coats dirty. If they don't care about having a dirty coat, I don't care either.

You also need to get your attitude in check when you get on my airplane and I inform you that our bins are full and I will need to check your bag. I say this to you not because I have decided that I don't like you, but because the bins are full, we are now checking bags, and I am very sorry. Sounds reasonable, right? Not so much. A normal scene goes something like this:

"What is your final destination?" I ask so I can tag your

bag properly.

"This is bullshit! My bags are regulation. They fit into the sizing bin! Why do I have to check my bags? What about the people before me with all of their damned luggage? Why don't you check their bags too?" the irate passenger yells (spitting, cussing, and causing a scene).

"Yes, Ma'am, we have been checking bags. Again, I need your final destination please."

"This is some bullshit, you know that? My destination is L.A.!"

"I will page you over the intercom with your baggage claim ticket number."

"Whoa! Now I have to go to baggage claim? This is just freaking unbelievable!"

How do I handle your outburst? I wait for you to leave, and then I smile and tell the operation's agent that your final destination is Seattle.

Another word of advice—you should watch your mouth when we are the ones responsible for checking your luggage because you might just get a nice surprise at baggage claim when you get to Los Angeles and your bags are in Seattle. Hehehe.

Chapter 6

My Hairy Dilemma

Once I got over my growing pains, the rest of my childhood was uneventful. Living in Texas, I had grown into a bonafide honor student who excelled in track. With my smarts, looks, and physical prowess, I was once again uber popular, but now I was also starting to attract the headache known as boys. The random knocks on my door drove my uncle nuts. I often found myself grounded for doing absolutely nothing other than attracting the "wrong attention". Over the years, my uncle calmed down and finally allowed me to date when I was sixteen.

I was rather mature for my age and my adopted parents decided that although I wasn't having sex it would be a good idea for me to get on birth control, just in case. I guess times were different back then. *Whatever*, I thought when we headed down to Planned Parenthood for an exam and a year's supply of pills in a pink case.

I was confused about the whole ordeal because I was not sexually active and unless you could get pregnant from dry humping through jeans, I was safe. But, what the hell, if it put my aunt and uncle at ease, so be it. I took the pills.

After about three months, I woke up, stumbled into the bathroom for my usual concoction of toothpaste dipped into the Arm and Hammer baking soda box, when I looked in the mirror and screamed, not just a regular scream, but a blood-curdling scream!

I had a fucking beard!!

My aunt came running up the stairs.

I turned to her, pointed at my neck and screamed, "I look like a fucking Bernstein Bear! What the hell happened?"

Even she had to scream. It was so shocking and horrific.

It turned out that the little pills in the pink case caused a hormonal imbalance in my body, producing extra hormones and extra hair growth.

I did what any normal girl with a sudden beard would do. I bought some shaving cream and a razor and, opting to skip the Old Spice, I got to work. From watching my uncle shave, I knew what to do, but it was a ghastly ordeal and only a temporary fix. I needed a solution, a permanent one.

Being a nerd, I knew my way around the library. I researched permanent hair removal and discovered electrolysis. I did not know it at the time, but electrolysis would soon become my obsession.

I found a part-time job working at Wendy's, home of the Texas double cheeseburger, in the food court at the mall. My family did not have much money, so my job provided me with not only a solution to my nightmare, but it also provided me with money for shopping. If I was going to be walking around with beard stubble, at least I could be fashionable.

After multiple phone calls and comparison of prices, I finally found my savior and her name was Teresa. During my second visit with her, while getting zapped, I learned that she only moonlighted part time as an electrologist. Her full-time job was as an American Airlines flight attendant!

Up to this point, all I wanted to do when I grew up was to become an accountant. I never considered being a flight attendant. I started looking forward to my bi-monthly appointments with Teresa and not merely to claim back my self-esteem. I was excited to hear her stories about the passengers she encountered while working first class and about how she would fly to Italy on a whim just to shop and eat! I often compared her tales to my aunt Claire's stories and it all sounded so glamorous, no matter what airline you worked for.

It was from Teresa that I first heard about Sun Airways. She talked about how they did not have first class service and said they didn't go to any exotic places. A fashionista like me, she also made fun of their uniforms, which were not nearly as polished as her own American Airlines uniforms were. I began to imagine wearing a swanky, fitted dress to work, flying all over the world, working in first class, partying with celebrities and meeting a rich husband. It sounded like such an amazing life. I made up my mind that if I ever chose that path, it would definitely be with American Airlines.

Chapter 7

Dear Diary,

Why do they always try to get one over on us?

I love Sun Airways even though I don't get to fly to all of the exotic places I dreamed about. Most of my flights are the same, and predictably pleasant, but I HATE working flights between the east coast and Florida. Once, I had just spent a twenty-hour overnight in New York with friends, and had the kind of fun where I literally arrived back at my hotel with thirty minutes to spare before having to be back in the lobby for my early morning flight to Miami. Boy, what a night!

Going through security, I was laughing with my crew-members and regaling them with details of my amaze-balls adventure. I was in great spirits as we approached our gate, but then I saw not one, not two, not three, but ten (count them . . . ten), wheelchairs already lined up waiting for us. There were also enough various breathing machines, catheter bags, canes, walkers, and oxygen tanks to supply a nursing home.

I looked at Diana, my fellow crewmember and rolled my eyes. "Oh shit! Damn it!"

"Oh girl, you are going to earn your money on this

flight!" She laughed.

I didn't find anything funny about the situation. I lost my smile and charisma and I was instantly pissed off. Before you go off on me, remember the title of this diary entry. I have absolutely nothing against people with disabilities, but I do have a beef with a couple of things that people with disabilities do.

THE HELP

I understand that you have serious health problems, but I will be perturbed if you show up with a catheter for your three-hour flight with no one to assist you and a note for me with instructions on what to do if your bag gets full.

Pardon me? I don't think so! There is not a single part of my training that says that I am a part-time, unpaid nurse and I don't take too kindly to being put on the spot. I hate to tell you this, but you are shit out of luck (no pun intended).

Why do disabled people refuse to check their bags, but always have the heaviest shit? What in the hell is in there, your entire medicine cabinet?

Earlier this year I had a man come aboard in a wheelchair sporting a cane and a bag. The man was twice my size but, of course, he still claimed he needed my help.

I gave his bag a small tug and it felt as heavy as bricks. "Sir, I am sorry, but your bag is way too heavy and I cannot, and will not, lift it for you. Did you know we offer checked bags for free? Would you like me to check yours for you?"

"No, I am not checking my bag! I have my medicine in

there and I need my bag with me," Mr. Wheelchair replied.

"Sir, you can take your medicine out of your bag before I check it."

"Oh, just give it to me. I can do it myself!" he said, grumbling.

See, I am smart. I knew he could lift his bag all along and that's how I know the majority of you think you can get one over on us. Most of you don't need any assistance at all, but you ask for it because you can board first, and you refuse to check your bag because you don't want to wait for it in baggage claim. What would the purpose be of using a wheelchair to pre-board only to have to wait for your luggage? Technically, people requiring wheelchairs are supposed to wait and deplane last so as not to hold up the more mobile passengers. How is it that so many of you, when we reach our destination, can suddenly walk just fine by yourselves? I didn't know we were in the business of healing, but damn we must carry some powerful water onboard!

EMOTIONAL ASSIST ANIMALS MY ASS

In my opinion, and I have a strong one on this topic, the Americans with Disabilities Act (ADA) has gone a bit too far with the emotional assist animal nonsense.

Again, hear me out. It is perfectly acceptable for you to have a guide dog if you are blind or visually impaired, or a dog that detects heart attacks, seizures and the like. These animals are trained and they work hard to save your life. An emotional assist animal is not trained and their owners have crossed the line and hide behind this act all too often. Because emotional assist animals fall under the ADA, people use it to circumvent having to pay for their pets to fly. This is where our Government could make some serious money if they were smart. Qualified assist animals always have a harness, a vest, or some type of paraphernalia stating that they have been properly trained, and they wear "please do not pet me" signs when they are working. If people had to pay for their so-called emotional assist animals, we would not see them anymore. I have seen "emotional assist" turtles, goldfish, rabbits. . . you name it, but this one takes the cake.

We had just landed in Los Angeles and we were en route to San Francisco. The ops agent came onboard and said, "Brace yourselves. There is a woman coming onboard with a monkey for an emotional assist animal."

"Whatchu talkin' about Willis? Run that by me again," I said, surprised anything could still manage to shock me.

"Supposedly, she has some emotional attachment to it and she has a doctor's note. She's protected by the ADA."

"That is some bullshit! Seriously?"

Sure enough, on comes the monkey . . . in a diaper.

I love cute, furry animals and I love monkeys when they are in the zoo, in cages because they can get crazy sometimes. But, no monkeys on planes should really be a new FAA rule.

This lady had the monkey sitting in her lap like a child. During boarding, people were doing double takes. Yeah, she is obviously crazy. Sorry folks, I wanted to say.

The monkey was okay until toward the end of boarding when he started shrieking. I was torn between cracking up and being pissed off because parents were freaking out, wondering if he was going to get loose and go ape shit. I was five seconds from having them removed from my flight when she took him into the restroom. When they came out, she gave him a treat and he calmed down. Fortunately, the remainder of the flight was quiet, just a bit weird.

SNEAKING PETS ONBOARD

If you are too broke or too cheap to pay for your pet to fly, then you probably should not have one.

I am going to assume that when you try to sneak your pet onboard that you just want to see if you can get away with it. Kudos to you if you caught a lazy flight attendant on your outbound flight, but on your way home, if you get me, look out. I can smell a rat 100 miles away. You may think you are clever for putting your pet inside of a regular bag, but did you ever think that people might wonder what the hell is wiggling around in there? Did you also stop to think that pet carriers have vents spaced throughout the bag so that your pet can breathe while regular bags do not? When I see you attempt to kill your pet by suffocating it in a bag, I'll turn you in to the ASPCA.

Confrontations with passengers about their illegally boarded pets are never pleasant.

"Excuse me, Ma'am, but what is moving inside of your bag?" I ask, already sure I know exactly what it is.

"Oh, it's just my . . . you know . . . ," the passenger replies with a wink, red in the face.

I am embarrassed because I called her out in front of other passengers until, as I begin to walk away, I hear a bark. "Excuse me, Ma'am, but I need to have a look inside of your bag. It not only seems to be moving, but now it is barking," I say, stopping dead in my tracks and turning back to her with narrowed eyes.

Without waiting for her to comply, I opened the bag to discover a mini Chihuahua going nuts. "Do you have a tag for your pet showing that you paid for it?"

"Oh, I am so sorry. I was too distracted and forgot."

I smile. "No worries, we are still at the gate. Let me get a supervisor down here so they can charge you for your pet and for a proper pet carrier."

I know when passengers pull stunts like this that they are full of it and I also know that they didn't "forget" to pay for their pet. One thing is sure, once a pet-smuggling passenger runs into me they will not try this dangerous stunt again.

EXPIRED COUPONS

Back in the day, we used to collect cash for alcoholic beverages. I loved working a Friday night flight into Las Vegas. Short on my rent? Not anymore! Before this flight, I could not pay my car note, but now I can. Thank you!

We had crafty ways of paying ourselves before paying the company until the company got tired of hearing that flight attendants were paying their mortgages and going on shopping sprees, so they decided you could only purchase alcoholic beverages with a drink coupon or a credit card. Then, we became the Bed, Bath and Beyond of the skies. It didn't matter if this was 2007 and you had a coupon from the 90's . . . we took it, until the higher ups became fed up with passengers constantly taking advantage of our kindness and they started printing coupons with expiration dates.

Our frequent flyers were given adequate notice of this change of policy. I will pardon you "once-a-year flyers", because you don't know any better. But you only get one pardon because by now you know the drill as well. I really hate that after two years into our new policy, I still have to set some of you straight.

"Can I get you something to drink?" I ask.

"Yes, I would like a gin and tonic." You hand me a very old coupon.

"Sir, we cannot take coupons that have expired."

"Well, they took it on the last flight," you tell me, wearing a look that says you are affronted, as if you had no clue and I am picking on you.

Maybe they took your expired coupon on your last flight because you got a nice flight attendant who, when you gave her that same tired line, took pity on you. But guess what? My niceness just went out of the window, as I am positive that by now you are fully acquainted with our new policy. You are a business flyer and you have pulled that stunt one too many times, and I am over you trying to pull a fast one!

"I find that hard to believe, Sir. We changed our policy two years ago. So if you don't have a valid coupon, I'll need to take your credit card please."

Slyly, you put away your coupon and produce a stack of valid, new coupons. Interesting. Aren't you tired of this lame-ass game and getting embarrassing looks from your fellow passengers? I guess you have zero shame. Just so you know, it makes you look really, really cheap to have to stoop so low for a drink that costs a measly $5. Non-alcoholic beverages are complimentary you know.

FREE DRINKS

We really take customer service to another level by showing our passengers just how much we appreciate their business. If you are lucky enough to travel with us on a holiday, we always offer you a free alcoholic beverage. When we have extended delays due to mechanical issues, we sometimes offer you a free alcoholic beverage to show you that we appreciate your patience. We even take it a bit further and extend the olive branch to include abnormal weather delays even though they are totally out of our control. So, why do you always try to take advantage of our kindness?

Until about three years ago, we did not have menus onboard to point out our special offerings and we took great pains not to make announcements about it either. But now, we offer menus that boast our offerings and you have caught on to us.

Once, I was working on Valentine's Day and had to prepare myself to deal with passengers and the free drinks that I knew we were going to offer. I asked a couple if they wanted a complimentary drink. The man ordered a Chardonnay, but the woman declined, explaining that she did not drink. Later, as I was offering seconds, the man ordered another Chardonnay, but told me it was for the woman, who was now sleeping. I told him I would bring her a drink later when she woke up. Honestly, we do not care if you are asleep or not. We will wake you up and make you take your drink. But I knew he was lying. He then ordered the wine for himself and I charged him for it. He acted indignant toward me for charging him and then opted for the free water.

Remember earlier, I said we would kindly offer you a drink? That means that you only get one free alcoholic beverage and that you are expected to pay for any future alcoholic beverages. I would have given him the second glass of wine free if he had not tried to get one over on me. Do you think when you go to a bar that they are going to give you free drinks for the fun of it? Unless you have established a rapport as a regular and you are a big tipper, the bartender is trying to flirt with you, or some stranger in the bar is picking up your tab, you are expected to pay for every drink you order. So why do you come onboard my flights and act as if you are not aware of this? Here are a few tips to help you receive free drinks onboard a plane:

1. After you order your first drink, give your flight attendant a tip (and I am not talking about lip service. Money talks and BS walks . . . catch my drift?) If you pay a cash tip that is at least the same value as your drink, you are guaranteed a "buy one get one

free" situation. For example, if you buy a drink for $5 and tip the flight attendant $5, you and your travel mates will continue to receive free drinks for the duration of the flight.

2. Be complimentary to us, and be sincere about it. If you strike up a conversation and you are interesting, I will definitely take care of you.

3. Side with us when you know a passenger is in the wrong and offer to help us with the situation. Just knowing that we have support from you will secure you free alcohol.

We have free rein over the alcohol and can give out as many free drinks as we like at our discretion, but when you ask, (especially if I am your flight attendant) you are surely going to pay for it.

I was on a flight once when everyone was frustrated due to a two-hour weather delay. I was extremely pissed too because I had to cancel dinner plans because of our inconvenient delay. As I was walking through the cabin, I encountered a pompous jerk of a businessman.

Putting his important business call on hold, he yelled, "HELLO? How much longer are we going to be delayed here, little lady? I have an important deal to close in a few hours and I need to let my investors (he pointed to the phone) know what is going on here."

Not caring who he was trying to impress on the other end of his phone call, I said, "Sir, I am not sure, but if you look outside your window, it does not look as if it is going to be anytime soon."

"Oh, that's just fucking great! Fucking unbelievable! Can't you do anything?" he screamed.

"I beg your pardon, Sir, but you need to watch your language or this weather delay will be the least of your worries. And no, there is nothing I can do, but sit here like you and wait."

I heard some snickering from a few rows as I walked away, leaving him with his smart-ass mouth hanging open, knowing I had impressed his caller and everybody else sitting around him. Finally, we took off and the pompous jerk moved to my section.

"Sir, can I get you anything to drink?" I asked him politely.

"The least you can do is give me a free drink!"

He was right. It was the least I could do, and I wasn't going to do it. However, his seatmates who had been kind to me, asked me nicely for a drink, and thanked me, would get free drinks. Mr. Pompous Businessman had to pay, and I think I even "accidentally" charged him for a double. He-hehe.

Sometimes, passengers take things a bit far in their quests for free drinks. When you go to a bar and you order a drink, and you don't like that drink, sometimes the bartender will replace it with something else. However, you do not get to consume the entire beverage and then claim you did not like it.

"Miss, I really did not like that Bloody Mary you served me."

I laughed because I was sure she was joking. "Well, I

can't tell because your cup is empty."

Shaking her head, she replied, "No, I really did not like that drink and I would like for you to comp me a drink for my inconvenience."

"I beg your pardon? You do not get to consume the entire drink and then ask me to comp you another one. I will need your credit card or a drink coupon, Ma'am."

Don't give me that look and stop trying to get over on me, because I am not falling for the banana in the tailpipe.

Chapter 8

Screw College

I excelled academically in high school, and by the time I graduated, I was beardless and excited about my transition into college. And that's when things went sideways in my life. As smart as I was, I didn't see any of it coming.

In college, sitting in the packed auditorium, trying to take adequate notes for my finance class, the last thing on my mind was my career. I was upset because, by the time I had finally made it to class, all of the seats in the front rows had already been taken. Stuck all the way in the back, I couldn't understand a word of what Mr. Gupta was saying. The extra chattering at the rear of the classroom made it even harder to concentrate. Halfway through class, my frustration reached an all-time high.

I raised my hand. "Mr. Gupta, are you saying that if I want to avoid paying taxes, I can place my money in a Swiss bank account?" I liked that idea, but had a feeling it was more complicated than that.

Mr. Gupta bobbed his head up and down. "No."

"Isn't that illegal?" I asked, wanting to be sure, confused

by the head bob that didn't match the words coming out of his mouth.

Mr. Gupta bobbed his head again. "No."

"Mr. Gupta, I'm confused. I just asked you two questions and you keep nodding your head "yes", but saying, "no". Which is it? Yes or no, Sir?"

The class erupted into giggles, because he did have the whole bobblehead thing going, but I was very serious.

Unfortunately, Mr. Gupta thought I was being a class clown and sent me to the Dean's office.

Shit! I had just gotten off academic probation and my average in Mr. Gupta's class was barely passing. I knew I could be in serious trouble and that I needed to weigh my options. Up until now, I had always been gifted academically. Yes, I was a nerd. It wasn't until I went to college that things began to go awry.

I graduated from High School in 1994 and off to college I went. Initially, when I went to college, I wanted to become an accountant. I know we have all been here, so I am not embarrassed to say that within my first semester my major changed to finance. I found myself weighing the pros and cons of going to class vs. attending to my social calendar. The calendar usually won out, and soon my major changed again.

Because I was finally in college, I felt as if I had to up the ante of "coolness". So I discovered this little green plant known as cannabis. The cannabis made me silly, and I found myself dissolving into fits of laughter every day for no good reason at all. After about two weeks, I stopped the drug use because ladies should not walk around with a cloud of cannabis wafting behind them . . . as if!

With no parental guidance or curfew, the remainder of my freshman year was spent living it up. I partied first and studied last, and at the beginning of my sophomore year, I ended up on academic probation. My aunt Melanie staged an intervention. After our counseling session, I had some serious thoughts to contemplate. I really needed to figure out what I wanted in life and how I was going to go about achieving my goals. Theoretically, I only had two more years to go before I graduated with my bachelor's degree, so I vowed to get back on the right path and to get my act together.

I still didn't quite know what I wanted to do in life, but I often found myself thinking about a career as a flight attendant. I remembered my aunt Claire's stories about the places she had traveled, the things she did on her overnights and all of the celebrities she had met. Her career sounded like so much fun, not at all boring like accounting classes.

Wanting to feel more secure about the remainder of my time in college, I tried to transfer out of Mr. Gupta's class, but we were nearing midterms and it was too late. His accent was so thick that I had no idea what in the hell he was saying half the time. I frequently nodded off in class with my tape recorder going.

We only had two tests for the whole semester, and I thought (with my tape-recorded sessions) that I was fully prepared to ace it. Then I received my grades and ended up with a "D"! That was the straw that broke the camel's back.

After class emptied out, I sat in my chair staring at the blackboard and pondering my options. With tears streaming down my face, I got out of my seat. I slowly approached the blackboard and pounded my head for inspiration. After none came, I said to myself, "Fuck this shit. I'll be a flight attendant!"

Ah, the innocence of youth. I still had no idea what was in store for me someday.

Chapter 9

Dear Diary,

Hey, Chunky Monkey?

S afety regulations of the U.S. Federal Aviation Administration (FAA) mandate that passengers must be able to lower their armrests and sufficiently buckle and fasten their seat belts. The average seat width for a domestic, economy flight ranges from 17"-19". Because over 30% of the U.S. adult population suffers from obesity, airlines are now trying to find ways to accommodate heavier passengers. Some major airlines have adopted a "passenger of size" policy that mandates that obese people have to buy an extra seat. Other airlines are considering charging a "fat tax"—an extra fee for overweight passengers who require extra fuel to travel around the world. Every airline has had to find tactful ways to handle this situation. My airline says that if you are ridiculously obese, you must buy a second seat. If you are just obese, you can borrow a seat belt extension.

BUYING AN EXTRA SEAT

The purpose of charging you for an extra seat is not to embarrass you because, let's face it, we did not put you in the situation that you are currently in, but rather to make other passengers of normal size comfortable and to make you comfortable as well.

I have worked many flights where we were completely full and the only seat available was between two obese passengers. Sadly, the normal sized passenger had to sit in the middle seat and it was a very unpleasant experience for that person.

When you purchase a ticket to fly, you purchase a full seat and the space underneath the seat in front of you for your legs and for your luggage. What you don't buy is half a seat or the body parts of another person spilling into your seat. This is why most airlines have adopted a "passenger of size" policy. This policy has deemed that if you cannot physically fit in the seat provided to you with the armrest lowered you must buy another seat. Look on the bright side, you are guaranteed that nobody sits next to you and ensuring that you can stretch out and take up as much room as you want without enduring the evil glares from a pissed-off passenger who's stuck sitting next to you.

Seat belt Extensions

Usually when a passenger of "generous size" boards my flight, they ask me for a seat belt extension. We are supposed to hand them one, tactfully. I do follow this rule . . . sometimes.

A year ago, I was working a flight from Dallas to Oklahoma City. Upon boarding, a passenger asked for a seat belt extension. When I checked my compartment, I only had one extension, the one we used for our demonstrations. I kindly told the passenger that I would have to check with the flight attendants in the rear of the aircraft because I did not have any available seat belt extensions. She said okay and proceeded to her seat. I called to the back and located another extension and I promised the passenger that I would have it for her soon. I got busy and forgot to hand the lady her seat belt extension (it was an honest mistake. I swear!). The front doors closed and I made the announcement to secure the cabin, turn off devices . . . yada, yada, yada.

As I began to do my walk through the cabin, I noticed her seat belt hanging out into the aisle. "Ma'am, we are on an active taxiway. Would you please fasten your seat belt?"

As I began to walk to the next row, I heard, "Well, if you had given me my damned extension, I would be buckled in, Bitch!"

Why, oh why, did she have to go and get all ghetto on me?

I stopped, put the fake smile on my face, made a pivot in the middle of the aisle, and said rather loudly, "Oh, I am so sorry I forgot your seat belt extension (I said those words extra loud). Let me get that for you, Ma'am." I made a big production (to quite a few snickers) of showing her how to attach the device.

I know right now you are simultaneously laughing and thinking I am mean, but again, to passengers like this I say don't get an attitude with me because of your situation. It's not my fault.

In this case, the passenger was very kind to me for the rest of the flight. She even took our seat belt extension with her to save herself the embarrassment on her return flight.

OWWE (OVER WING WINDOW EXIT) SEATING

It is no secret that the OWWE seats are some of the most coveted seats in coach/economy class. While the seats are the same size, the legroom is plentiful for people over a certain height so they can stretch their legs without catching a cramp. The OWWE is an exit door and in the event of an evacuation, you could be the first person out the door. Technically, the idea behind your sitting in the exit row is for you to help evacuate passengers.

There are certain things that can prevent you from sitting in this area—if a child is under the age of fifteen, if you pre board the flight, if you have a device like crutches that could hinder you from being able to assist in evacuating the aircraft, if you have an animal (because they are like children), if you do not speak or understand English, or if you need a seat belt extension, you cannot sit in the OWWE. The FAA has strict guidelines that must be adhered to regarding the OWWE and one of those guidelines says, "A passenger seated in an exit seat must NOT require a seat belt extension to fasten his seat belt." An exit seat means having direct access to an exit without passing around an obstruction. And you, Chunky Monkey, with that seat belt extension are an obstruction.

If you require a seat belt extension, chances are you may not physically fit through the exit door. Therefore, you are blocking the exit, rendering it unusable, and could possibly cause some fatalities in the event of an emergency. Have you ever noticed that the OWWE doors are a fraction of the size of the door that we use to board our flights? Well, the next time you are on a flight, pay attention.

On one flight, I saw a passenger trying to act nonchalant as he made a beeline for the OWWE. I was standing there acting as if I was bored and did not have a care in the world, but that is where I fooled him because I knew he could not possibly fit in the seat without assistance, and I wanted to see just what he would do. I faced the forward portion of the aircraft and watched him using my peripheral vision. He was sweating and looked to see if I would notice as he slyly took a stolen seat belt extension out of his suitcase and quickly tried to connect it.

I whipped my head around so fast, that my hair extensions slapped me in the face. "Sir, I am sorry, but was that a seat belt extension I just saw?"

"Yes, I need it because I cannot get the seat belt around me."

"It is perfectly fine to use a seat belt extension; however, you may not sit in the OWWE while using one," I told him nicely.

Don't look at me as if this is new to you, because I know you know better. You are just mad that you were busted was what I wanted to say.

My own personal requirement for the OWWE is that people don't try to squeeze into them illegally. Sir, I need you to stop lifting your fat! Yes, you who could not get the seat belt properly around your waist so you looked around and, when you did not see me, lifted your tummy to buckle that belt. I am pissed that you have outdone me and now legally, I have no right to move you, but honestly, that's just plain gross!

I want you to stop kicking, moving around in your seat, and continually stretching your seat belt to the very end, because these are not jeans, honey. They don't stretch.

When people pull this trick they eventually get red in the face, sweat beads on their forehead and threatens to run down their face and onto the collar of their white shirt. They feverishly adjust the air vent and then have the audacity to look at me and ask, "Why is it so hot in here?" as if they really want me to answer that.

I also want you to stop stealing the legroom in the OWWE and save it for the people who NEED it. So, when you are 5'2", Miss Selfish, there is no need for you to occupy the seat with the most legroom on the entire plane! I see you avoiding eye contact with the man who is 6'6" and really NEEDS that seat with all of that legroom. Shame on you for being so selfish and ignorant.

HAVE THE BATHROOMS GOTTEN SMALLER?

I was asked this question while I was in the back galley minding my own business, and I almost choked on my water.

Hmmm . . . let me see, I guess the smallness of the bathroom has absolutely nothing to do with the fact that maybe you have gotten bigger? The bathrooms on the aircraft are just a fancier version of the port-a-potties that you find at an outdoor concert. Albeit, the bathrooms on the plane are a tad cleaner, but the size has not changed.

"Buddy, you just hate fat people," my friend Veronica said to me once.

That was a bit harsh, as I do not hate any particular group of people, unless you belong to a hate group and, to be honest, I do have a healthy friend or two. However, I can dislike some fat people all I want and I'll tell you why.

I dislike the ones who think it's appropriate to take three 100-calorie snacks and then order a Diet Coke. Kind of defeats the purpose, don't you think?

I dislike the ones who sneer at me when I complain about needing to lose five pounds. Hey, at least I know my limits.

I dislike the fact that because of a lack of self-control, some develop a myriad of health problems that my healthy self has to pay for. Thanks, health insurance!

I dislike that some are irresponsible, stuffing their faces and then going and getting a lap-band procedure paid for by their insurance company, but when I inquire about getting liposuction I'm told I'd have to pay out of pocket. Where is my damned help?

I dislike when someone sues an airline for discrimination because their "fatness" falls under the ADA. What the hell?

And I really dislike that I had to write this chapter to point out the silly things people do on my plane, therefore causing me to lose my cool and telling you all how I really feel.

But, hey, somebody has to. Hehehe.

Chapter 10

Becoming a Flight Attendant

I could not stick around college for another two years, so I opted to get my Associate's Degree. After receiving my Associate's Degree, I applied to be a flight attendant with American Airlines and Sun Airways (Sun Airways is, of course, not a real airline, but I have to protect my ass). Working for American Airlines, in first class, traveling all over the world and meeting lots of celebrities, sounded so glamorous and right up my alley.

None of this applied to Sun Airways. But they had received numerous accolades and had always been touted as the best airline to work for. So I really could not go wrong with either choice. I submitted my application to both airlines and eagerly awaited an invitation to interview.

American Airlines called first, and I thought I was in heaven! I showed up for my interview in a freshly dry-cleaned suit with a smile plastered on my face, ready to wow the interviewer with my charm. When I got to the room, I realized that I would not have a one on one interview. Instead, we were arranged around the room in a roundtable formation. The interview was to be conducted in a group style, giving me a sudden case of stage fright. Still, everything seemed to be going well, until I noticed Cindy. Cindy must have had some kind of a nervous syndrome because occasionally, she would hop out of her seat as if it was too hot. She would calm down and then begin to swat at her hair as if a bug was buzzing around her head. I kept looking out of the corner of my eye to see if anybody else noticed her odd behavior. Cindy thoroughly distracted me throughout the entire interview process. I left feeling very disappointed that I hadn't done a better job.

Within a month, I heard from Sun Airways. Again, I got gussied up and ready for my interview. I ended up having three individual interviews that day and was confident that I had done well.

After about two months of waiting, I received a phone call from Sun Airways inviting me to a training class. At this point, I still had not received anything from American Airlines, though my hopes were still up. I accepted the invitation to attend training with Sun Airways and thought, what the heck. Why not?

I received a packet from the airline instructing me to learn PAs (public announcements) before class. Being the nerd that I am, I did just that. At stoplights, working out on the treadmill, even during bathroom breaks, you would find me memorizing and rehearsing my lines. By the time training rolled around, I was very good at my PAs and ready for my moment to shine on the first day of training. I thought we'd have to deliver our PAs before class started, in order to weed out the students who did not care enough to read their packet. But we didn't do our PAs that morning or even that afternoon. By the end of the day, I was confused, so I raised my hand and asked if we were going to do our PAs. I was told (laughingly, and with a wave of a hand) that while we should be prepared, we were not actually going to go over them for at least two weeks. I was pissed because there were a few people I knew who would not have passed the test that first day, and I wanted them gone! They were not taking training as seriously as I was, and it wasn't fair that I had spent my precious time in the bathroom rehearsing for no reason.

As a civilian, you may not be aware that being a flight attendant is more than passing out drinks and food. We learn safety drills for evacuations, how to perform CPR and rescue breathing, the Heimlich maneuver, and various first aid treatments. Only a very small portion of the training is focused on actual inflight service.

After about five weeks of training, I graduated from the course. I was so happy! Looking back at my class photo, I look like the biggest dork ever in my uniform. Our uniforms did not come close to looking as polished and professional as American Airline's uniforms and though I was thoroughly disappointed, I had to work with what was provided so don't fault me. Now, there's a diva in the house, but it took some time.

About a week after I finished training with Sun Airways, American Airlines called and invited me to their training program. What the hell? *Oh well, it's too late*, I thought. Training was stressful enough and, more importantly, I was in a financial pickle. I was broke. My bank account could not take another beating so I declined the offer. I did not know at the time if that was the best decision for me and I wrestled with that choice for a while.

For the first two years after I became a flight attendant, I relished my ability to travel all over the US. I partied like a rock star. What, there's a party in Las Vegas tomorrow? I am there!

I had a few guys in different cities and was having a blast. Side note: having guys in multiple cities is the biggest flight attendant myth. While a very small percentage of flight attendants and pilots do practice this, most of us have families or are in monogamous relationships.

I was living the high life. My friends back in college were envious that I had found a career I loved. What could possibly go wrong?

Chapter 11

Dear Diary,

Where are their manners?

A typical flight attendant's schedule is usually about three days on and four days off. That means we work for three days a week and we're off for four days a week.

I, on the other hand, work about five or six days a week with one or two days off. I am a workaholic and because I am topped out (meaning I have reached the maximum in pay), the money is freaking awesome! I do not have any kids, so I am free to earn as much as my little heart desires. Because I work so much, there are just some days when I am totally over it and want to scream. No matter how tired I am, I always try to be mindful of my manners. However, passengers don't, and I have had it up to here with them.

SPEAK WHEN SPOKEN TO

When we are children, most of our parents teach us the basics about good behavior and manners. My grandmother instilled in me that you should always speak when spoken to. To not do so would convey that you are either deaf, just plain rude, or that the speaker didn't talk loudly enough. In some cases, I'm sure it's rudeness.

The other day, I was boarding a flight and I began with my usual, "Good morning! Welcome aboard, how are you?" The first ten passengers greeted me with similar responses and then one came onboard, looked at me, and then looked away. I wondered if maybe I was not speaking loudly enough, but doubted that was the case since the passenger was right there, close enough for me to smell his cologne. *Maybe he's just having a bad morning*, I thought.

On the next flight, I tried it again, only this time I had my Captain stand with me because he could not believe that I was speaking to people and being met with silence. This time, I had a nice pattern going until I was hit with the blank, Asian stare. Okay, maybe she didn't understand English? Still, I carried on greeting people until the last passenger boarded. I was front and center with a smile plastered on my face until a man came aboard and avoided all eye contact with me. I offered him a greeting anyway, and was met with silence.

Now, I get it . . . if you board and do not make eye contact, then that's my cue that you do not want to be spoken to and that I should just shut up? Did I get that right? If so, I just want you to think about one thing—you have no idea how many times we have to stand there and offer greetings to you. Let's do the math. If I work three flights today and each flight has about sixty passengers onboard, that totals about 180 greetings just from me alone. So guess what? I am tired of greeting you and saying goodbye to you, but I do it anyway. The least you could do is indulge me, if not with a word, then a smile would be nice. Thank you!

ONBOARD MANICURES AND PEDICURES

One day, I was sitting on my jumpseat when I started hearing this "click-click" noise. I sat still for a bit, wondering what it was. The noise stopped and I went back to reading my book. It began again and then it dawned on me . . . it was a nail clipper I heard.

I got up to investigate the culprit and came across a businessman in the front row. He was sitting behind the forward bulkhead (partition), so I did not see him until I rounded the corner. Even though I knew the sound of nail clippers when I heard them, I was still not prepared for what I saw. Mr. Nail Clippers was sitting there with his socks off, clipping his damned toenails and dropping them on the floor! Ewww!

I got major attitude. "Sir, you cannot clip your toes on an aircraft! We have OSHA (Occupational Safety and Health Administration) laws and that is deemed unsanitary!"

I'm positive clipping your nails on an airplane does not fall under OSHA, but it sounded legal and it scared him, which was what I wanted. I gave him a bag to clean up his clippings and waited until he put his socks and shoes back on.

If you are on my flight, my make-believe OSHA laws will apply to those of you who try to polish your nails onboard too. Really, you couldn't find time before you boarded the flight to polish your nails? Toxic fumes are not fun on airplanes though they do help me sniff you out when, after I asked you to put your nail polish away, you sneak it out again. Behavior like this is why I grin from ear to ear when your offending nail polish explodes in your Louis Vuitton bag. Mission accomplished!

TALKING WHILE CHEWING

When I was a child, I remember having dinner with my parents one night and asking my dad a question. As I was chewing my food, I opened my mouth to speak and I damned near was smacked in my mouth for it. Why? Because you are not supposed to talk with food in your mouth. Nobody wants to see the disintegrated particles in your mouth or, even worse, food falling out.

Nothing disgusts me more than coming by to offer someone a drink while they are chewing peanuts. When Mr. Peanut opens his mouth, I see things I really don't want to see and then those nasty crumbs fall out onto his shirt and our tray table and I wrinkle my nose in disgust because he obviously didn't know to cover his mouth.

So please, please cover your mouth. I am asking you nicely.

While we are on the topic of talking while chewing, please keep in mind that this also applies to bubble gum. As a kid, I loved bubble gum, especially Big League bubble gum. I loved smacking and blowing bubbles, until one day as I was smacking away, my dear grandmother held out her hand and made me spit my gum into it. I asked her why she made me spit my gum out. She said I was not raised in a barn, it's rude to smack gum, and blow bubbles while in the company of others. I did not get what she meant until I was older. If I hear someone smacking gum onboard, it irritates me like fingernails on a chalkboard. I really find it offensive when I am asking you for your drink order and you have the audacity to blow a bubble in my face before telling me you would like a Sprite. A bit of advice . . . unless you are a child, blowing bubbles and smacking gum is never, ever acceptable.

VENDING MACHINE

My airline company loves you so much that we are supposed to give you everything you ask for within reason. But because of your constant abuse of this policy, I have now enacted my own rules. If you ask for a drink that comes in a can, expect it to be opened for you.

I was taking drink orders one day when a lady asked for a can of Coke. "Sure, no problem," I said.

About thirty minutes later, she asked for a can of orange juice. Again, no problem. I started to get suspicious when I realized she never wanted a cup or ice and that whenever I came through my section to collect trash, she never had any trash to give me. I thought maybe the other flight attendants had collected her trash, so I asked them only to learn they had not been in my section. *Hmmm . . . that's odd*, I thought.

I forgot about it until about two hours into the flight when I saw her go to the back and get another can of soda from one of the other flight attendants. That's when I realized she wasn't drinking the drinks; she was just stashing them in her bag.

So, I did what any curious flight attendant would do, and I approached her. "Ma'am, I am sorry, but whatever service items we give you must be consumed on the aircraft. You may not take any items except the snacks or the onboard magazine with you."

"I don't have any service items. I drank all of the cans I got from you," she said.

I knew she was lying, but I had to maintain my professional demeanor. I was just about to walk away, when the passenger seated next to her said, "Miss, she has all of the cans in her bag. Look, one just fell out."

I looked at the can-stealing passenger.

"Oh, did I do that?" she asked, trying to act all innocent.

We are not vending machines and it is highly inappropriate for you to think that you are going to get away with this sort of thing on my watch. I need to do my part to protect our profits after all.

PUT THE TOILET SEAT DOWN

Gentlemen, this one is for you. This one really chaps my hide because I have brothers, and I know you guys were taught this simple task when you were kids. Why, as an adult, you don't care to put the toilet seat down is beyond me, but I am tired of your not caring. I constantly have to remind my boyfriend to put the seat back down. He thinks it's cute, but he doesn't know that I charge him a dollar every time I have to remind him and steal it from his wallet when he's not looking.

About five years ago, while I was working, I had to pee so bad that just the thought of sneezing made me want to wet my pants. As soon as I finished my service, I started doing "the dance" outside the occupied lavatory. When a man came out, I quickly ran in and sat without looking (I will tell you later why I sat . . . I know, totally gross!) and I fell into the toilet! I was so mortified that I cried and almost called in sick for the rest of my flights because I was sure I had contracted Hepatitis A, B, and C.

You should NEVER sit on a public toilet without some form of cover on the seat protecting you. I definitely know better, but I did not have time to adjust my "lady parts". Walking around in tights and thongs all day can really twist a girl up so, if we have to go, we need to make sure we have time to adjust.

After graduation, I was so excited finally to be working an actual flight on a real airplane. Before service, I had to use the onboard lavatory. I went in and squatted over the seat. I could tell I was going, but I didn't hear anything hit the toilet water. Instead, I realized, urine was running down my legs and into my new tights. What the hell? Looking down, I saw that my "parts" were in a jam and I realized that I had neglected to adjust. Let me tell you, there is nothing worse than walking around with pee on your legs and in your tights for a six-hour workday. And that is why, when I don't have time to adjust, I make sure to sit.

Let me ask you something. Why do some of you come to the airport, sit in the waiting area for hours, only to come on-board the plane and blow up my bathroom with your stink? Nothing makes me more nauseous than encountering your morning bowels on my plane. Come on, Dude, it's 5:00 AM! Were all of the restrooms out of order at the airport? No? Then your behavior is just plain rude and, the minute you walk out of the lavatory, I will make a big display of spraying air freshener and will give you dirty looks for the rest of the flight.

SHITTY PANTS

We've all seen passengers who are too big to fit into the lavatories onboard airplanes. While I cannot relate to their dilemma, it would be nice if they tried hard to squeeze into the lavatory. If that doesn't work, they need to try their best to hold it until we land and they can go in the terminal. Think happy thoughts or whatever it takes, but for crying out loud, don't shit your pants.

I was the lead flight attendant on a flight one day from Chicago to Cleveland. Just when I thought we had finished boarding, a lady came running down the jet bridge with four kids in tow. I directed them to the back of the plane where there was enough room for her and all of her family and I watched as she attempted to walk down the aisle. When she realized she could not fit, she turned sideways and did an awkward little shuffle down the aisle all the way to the back of the plane. During the flight, she took one of her kids to the bathroom, but she could not fit in the lavatory either, so she left the door open and exposed us all to the unwelcome sight of her child using the bathroom. Thanks a lot! When the child finished, the mom needed to go and attempted once more to close the door to no avail. She tried turning different angles and still had no luck. Embarrassed, she finally gave up and went back to her seat. As we were making our final descent into Cleveland, I was picking up trash and, when I got near her, I smelled an awful stench. I had no idea what her child had been eating, but the smell was rank. She waited until all the other passengers left the plane before she got up and filed out with her family. Even after she was gone, the smell lingered. It was so bad that I had to put my head in an airsick bag just to breathe. As we were cleaning up the cabin, I noticed a wet stain on the seat she had occupied. Since I was the one to find it, I had to clean it up. As I got closer, I realized the stain was not juice, or water or pee, but a wet stain left from her having shit her pants! *Screw cleaning up that mess*, I thought, opting instead to make a note to let the maintenance crew know to replace the entire seat cushion. Come to think of it, maybe I should have saved that special seat cushion for a passenger I didn't like!

ME SPEAKING NO ENGLISH

The one thing I relish more than anything is kicking you off my flight when you deserve it. When I get the opportunity to have someone ejected, I rejoice in my power.

Two years ago, I was working a flight from Chicago to Philadelphia. We were running late and, toward the end of boarding, an Asian family of six came onboard. The family consisted of a husband, a wife, three kids, and grandma. They did not have seats together so the wife approached another passenger and asked if he and his daughter would move to accommodate her and her kids. I was not too happy with this because the gentleman had boarded early and he had every right to his chosen seat.

Prior to boarding, the Operations Agent had told us that we'd have a family named Phuong with a lap child on the flight. A lap child is a child two years old or younger, who can fly free. If there happens to be an extra seat, the child can occupy that seat, but if not the child must be on their parent's lap. In this case, since the flight was full, Phuong's child was going to have to sit in one of their parent's laps.

Seeing no kids on laps, I asked Mrs. Phuong if her daughter was a lap child.

"She no lap!" Phuong insisted.

The manifest was clear. On this particular flight, only one lap child was listed, named Phuong.

"Ma'am, I need to check your ID because it says here that your child is supposed to be a lap child."

She shook her head. "I no id. She no lap."

"Ma'am, you had to have some form of ID to board the aircraft."

"My hu-band (no, that's not a typo), he have ID," Phuong insisted.

I approached her husband and asked him for some kind of identification. *Poor thing, it's clear he didn't wear the pants in his family*, I thought. Sure enough, the name on the driver's license he gave me matched the name on my manifest!

I approach Mama Phuong again. "Ma'am your ID matches my manifest and it says here that your child is a lap child. You will need to sit the child on your lap or we will put you on another flight. We don't have any seats to spare on this one."

"I no move!" she insisted, wearing a mulish look.

At this point, even the other passengers had had enough. You just really don't want to mess with the east coast.

"Kick that bitch off of this plane!" someone yelled.

"We need to go! We're already an hour late!" another passenger shouted.

I lost my patience with Phuong. "Ma'am, this is your last chance. If you don't move, I will have your entire family removed from this flight."

"I no move!" she replied.

Now, I was royally pissed off. No way was this lady going to come on my flight, undermine my authority, and refuse to comply with the rules. I conferred with my crew and then called security. It really was for their own safety that they were removed because I'm sure they would have suffered bodily harm from the other passengers had they stayed

When the cops came onboard, they told her to get her stuff and get off the plane.

"No! Please, please . . . I am sorry. We will move now."

Oh, now you can speak English? And now you want to move? *Too late*, I thought.

At the point when the cops are called, you have used your last lifeline and have no choice but to vacate the aircraft. Your pleas will be ignored, just like Phuong's. I felt bad for the grandma because she truly did not speak English and was very confused about the whole situation.

As they left, I was smiling with glee. I bet that lady never gave a flight attendant a hard time ever again. Hehehe.

Chapter 12

9/11 . . . the Day Everything Changed

On September 11, 2001, I was staying at my girlfriend Tinsley's house when my phone rang. I was enjoying my sleep, so I didn't answer. When the phone just kept ringing, I knew something was wrong.

My mom started to have a complete meltdown as soon as she heard my voice, and this freaked me out. She kept asking where I was and if I was okay. Finally, after assuring her, that I was okay, I asked her what all the fuss was about.

"Oh my God, you haven't heard?" she said.

"Heard what? What is going on?

"A plan was hijacked and crashed into the World Trade Center."

I hung up, in shock. Tinsley and I watched the horrific events unfold in front of us and, as we were watching, the second plane crashed into the World Trade Center. I threw up, thinking that what we had seen couldn't be real. When I realized that we had just watched a live airplane crash, I immediately tried to contact all the people I knew at American Airlines and Sun Airways to find out where they were and if they were okay. Fortunately, I didn't know anybody involved in the crashes, but it was still a very emotional time for my inflight family and me.

In training, we are taught self defense and how to secure a bomb and we're given codes to use if we are subjected to a hijacking, but nothing prepares you for an actual hijacking and it is terrifying. These people showed up for work expecting a normal day. Some were probably angry at their spouse or their kids, making plans for their overnight or making plans for their return trip home that they were never going to make. As a civilian, you do not realize that while our job is fun and comes with amazing perks, we put our lives on the line every time we step on an aircraft because we have no idea what our day will hold. We pray for a safe return home every day.

The aftermath of 9/11 prompted some serious changes within every airline and airport. Attitudes were different too among employees and passengers. Now, passengers were willing to be quiet and listen to our safety demonstrations instead of the usual, "This again? I have seen this 1,000 times," attitude. Everybody was on high alert, giving neighbors accusatory looks, scanning everybody from top to bottom, and creating conspiracy theories. Of course, after a year, our good-old customers were back to their normal selves.

I no longer wrestled with my decision about choosing Sun Airways over American Airlines. In terms of pay, my airline always held the fifth and sixth spots respectively, but after 9/11, we moved to the number one spot and life was good once again! Our wonderful union negotiated an industry-leading contract and we strutted through the airport as if our shit smelled liked roses.

After about three years, something caused a change in me. I was tired of the hotel room parties where I would sip on one drink all night and watch everyone else plotting about who they wanted to spend the night with. It was quite entertaining at times, but I was tired of jet setting all over the country to see my "men", and I was tired of living out of my suitcase. Soon, I became known as a "slam clicker" (someone who declines to hang out with their crew or meet for dinner, and instead slams their door and clicks their light switch out). I guess I was a slam clicker, kind of. If I didn't feel that I would hang out with you in my normal life, then I didn't want to hang out with you at work. My moments alone became precious, and I no longer wanted to share those times with people who didn't interest me or were nosey flight attendants who asked too many personal questions. I always had my own agenda in each city and I had no problem going solo.

As our company began to grow, they started hiring flight attendants who made me skeptical about coming to work. This new batch of attendants was fat and lazy. They constantly complained about being on reserve and about going through what we all have to go through to gain seniority.

I grew sick of the constant negativity. I became more "black and white" and less "gray" as the months wore on. I knew within seconds if I would like you (and you knew it too). Regardless, I was always cordial and respectful. I didn't care to hang out too much in the gray areas, and I soon began to see who was fake and who was real. I also began to notice a change in our customers.

Chapter 13

Dear Diary,

Hey, don't bust my balls. I'm just doing my job.

Other than dealing with all of the shenanigans you put us through, my job is an amazing career choice. I know many of you are jealous that I get to wake up in a different state each day and each week if I choose. I fly with completely different people all the time, while you sit in the same boring office, with the same boring people every day. While my job is incredible, it's still a job we must do with as little drama, eye rolling, and mouthing off as possible. Some days, that's asking a lot.

OWWE BRIEFING

If you fly frequently, and snag those emergency row seats with more legroom, you might become irritated that you have to watch us do the "dog and pony show" at the start of every flight. But federal law requires us to give you a safety briefing every flight to make sure you understand that you are sitting in the emergency exit row and to ensure that you are willing and able to assist in the event of an emergency evacuation. I understand you feel like a VIP when you sit in the OWWE. However, until the FAA issues you a card stating that you are exempt from our announcements, you must listen to us with your full attention.

"Ma'am, can you please disconnect your call so we can go over the briefing?" I asked a passenger once on a packed flight.

She rolled her eyes dramatically. "I already know what you are going to say and yes I am willing and able to assist! Okay?"

I totally wanted to smack her smart ass and dare her to try to give my briefing verbatim. Instead, I said, "While I do understand you probably do this every week, it is still my job to give this briefing."

Seriously, what prompts people to act this way? I am sure you have certain requirements of your job and would get pissy too if you were always met with an attitude just for doing what is required of you.

I really love the dilemmas at the OWWE sometimes, especially when a grandma approaches and swears she can lift fifty pounds. Really, lady? Because I am young and fit and every year, when I go through a refresher course on emergency evacuations, I have to lift that door. It's quite heavy for me, so I know you are a goner. But hey, my job is to ask if you are capable and if you choose to lie and say you are, so be it. My job is done.

Collecting Service Items

As a part of our duties as a flight attendant (steward, stewardess, or whatever title tickles your fancy), we serve you beverages and sometimes snacks onboard your flight. We give you these items knowing you are aware that, when we are in our final descent, all of the items we gave you must be collected. We come by to collect your trash as soon as we can.

You may not know this, but we have a certain order we follow when providing you services. Shortly (we all have our own definition of what this means) after takeoff, we come by and offer you a drink. Then, if available on your flight, we provide you with some type of snack. While you are consuming your beverage and snack of choice, we are organizing our galley and putting things back in order. We may take a short break to grab ourselves some food (because we get hungry too). Then, when we feel it has been long enough, we come by and pick up trash. Don't fret if you don't hear us walk by. We'll be back. There's no need for you to wag your cup at me. Doing so might make me wonder if you are panhandling for cash and that is illegal.

Please keep in mind that if we ask you for trash, we are asking you for ALL of your trash. Anything stuffed in your seat-back pocket (including dirty diapers, banana peels, apple cores, and nasty-ass dip cups), are considered trash. That newspaper that you demolished and threw on the floor? Trash. So, just give it to us already!

I had this interesting exchange on a flight recently.

"Ma'am, I need to collect your coffee cup for landing please," I said.

"No, it is full and I am just going to keep this so you don't get burned," the passenger replied, stubbornly holding on to their cup.

I must admit, that was a great comeback. For a second I was speechless, but only temporarily.

I smiled one of my fake smiles. "That's okay ma'am. I would rather I get burned than have you get hurt, so please hand me your cup. Thank you."

We have heard it all. Once, I even had a lady say she was keeping her ice for her daughter because she was having problems with her ears, but when I walked back through the cabin, the mom was chewing on the ice, and the baby was laughing. Yes, people will go that far to keep their ice. I know! Ridiculous.

We collect service items for safety reasons. Think about it. Your tray table has to be raised for landing, so where would you put your cup if we let you hang onto it? What if there was turbulence during landing and you choked on that ice you insisted on keeping? What if your can of Coke went flying and hit someone in the head? I'd know it was your fault, and you'd know it too, but that wouldn't stop you from filing a bogus lawsuit against my beloved airline.

Don't leave your crap on the floor for somebody (usually the flight crew and not some maid service) else to pick up. We remember who you are when you get off, and we cuss you behind your back and wonder just how dirty your house is. Judging by your habits, it's probably filthy. On really short flights, you definitely know better and I am going to need you to do more drinking and less socializing because when the time comes for me to collect I don't want you holding up your damned finger asking if I can come back. If you do that, our exchange will probably go something like this one I had recently:

"Ma'am, I need to collect your service items for landing please."

"Can you give me a minute? I need to finish my Diet Coke."

"No, I cannot give you another minute. I need to take my seat for my safety, and I need to collect service items right now."

"I'm sorry you hate your job." The passenger slowly handed me her cup.

"Oh no, sweetie, it's not my job I hate . . ." I said, trailing off on purpose, giving her a fake smile and walking away knowing she knew exactly what I had left unsaid.

SEAT BELT SIGN

When the seat belt sign is illuminated, you are to remain in your seat until it has been turned off.

Having the seat belt sign on is the same as being in a car with your seat belt on. Get it? Then why do I have to remind people about this constantly? If you are blind, then you are exempt from this rant, but the rest of you are not and you have no excuse. I will let you in on a little secret. The pilots (you know, the guys/gals who sit in the cockpit, the ones responsible for getting you from point A to point B safely) control that sign, not us lowly flight attendants. So stop asking when it is going to be turned off!

"Ma'am, can I go to the restroom?" a passenger asked me on a flight the other day.

"Sorry, but I cannot give you permission while the seat belt sign is on."

"Well, I need to go really bad." He squirmed in his seat. "Do you know when it's going to be turned off?"

"When the captain feels it's safe, he'll turn the fasten seat belt sign off."

"Do you know when that's going to be? Can you call him? I really have to go."

What are you, five years old? Read between the lines, people. I cannot give you permission because it is my job to obey the signs and to remind you of them. That's it. I am not a defensive end and I am not obligated to tackle you if you try to get up so if you have to go to the restroom for crying out loud, don't piss your pants at your seat like the lady in this next story.

The seat belt sign had been on for a long time due to some bad turbulence. The lady kept asking if she could go to the restroom. I told her several times that I could not give her permission because the fasten seat belt sign was illuminated. She looked as if she was going to burst her pants, but I could not tell her it was okay for her to get up. Finally, the flight smoothed out. I expected she would be the first person running for the restroom, but I never saw her go. I was not concerned because it was not my business and I had other things to worry about. When she exited the aircraft, she was very nice and told me to have a great day. The flight crew began to tidy up the aircraft and when we got to her row, we found a full airsick bag . . . and it was not full of vomit. I remembered the lady had worn a long skirt and when I put two and two together, I dry heaved. Yep. The passenger had apparently lifted her skirt and used the airsick bag as a potty while seated in her seat. It was an empty flight and she had a row to herself but still . . . nasty heifer.

We definitely use the seat belt sign to our advantage when passengers don't get the subliminal hints we give them when we want them to vacate our galley and leave us alone. Not noticing our one-word answers? Have you noticed we have not asked you one thing about yourself or that we're not laughing at your jokes? How about the fact that we raised our USA Today papers up to block you from being able to look at us? Still don't get it? Well, I will fix that. I'll just make a call to the pilot and . . . oh, the seat belt sign has just been turned back on. I am sorry, but you must return to your seat. Bye bye now!

STOWING LUGGAGE

Your inability to figure out how to stow your own luggage is a major pet peeve among all flight attendants.

YOU packed your bag and got it into your car. YOU rolled your bag from your car into the airport. YOU lifted your bag onto the conveyor belt at security. YOU managed your bag this entire time and now YOU get your ass on our planes and need assistance? I don't think so!

We are also very tired of having to tell you that if you have two carryon items, the smaller one needs to go underneath the seat in front of you while the larger one goes in the overhead bin. Large items include roller bags, garment bags, duffle bags, instruments, and anything else too big to stuff away. Smaller items include attaché cases, briefcases, shopping bags, and purses (yes, purses). It is an FAA requirement that all luggage is stowed properly for takeoff and landing. The cabin is not secure if luggage is sticking out into the aisle, if you have purses in your lap, bags in the seat, or if the overhead bins are open. If the cabin is not secure, we may have to delay takeoff because of your failure to understand this basic concept.

Did you know that if there is an emergency, and your luggage is not properly secure, you could be injured during an evacuation? You could trip over your luggage or your shoe could get caught on a strap.

You really cannot blame anyone else for your incompetence, but that doesn't stop some of you from writing letters to my company, telling them how rude I was (even though you are probably just like the passengers I have to remind several times to stow their stuff).

"Ma'am, can you please stow your handbag (fake Louis Vuitton) under the seat for takeoff?"

"I am not putting my purse on the floor!" you say, lips

quivering from the indignity of even the suggestion.

"Well, did you bring your dust bag?" I ask.

"What's a dust bag?"

I know she did not know this, but I saw that fake Louis Vuitton the minute she stepped onboard my flight and I knew I was going to have an issue with her and her fakeness. Here's what I wish I could have said to her when she gave me a hard time about putting her bag under the seat. "Sweetie, when you buy real, expensive bags, they come with what is called a dust bag to prevent your real, expensive bag from getting dirty or dusty. You and I both know your purse is fake, so please stop with the attitude because now people are looking and I would hate to embarrass you any further."

In a previous chapter, I mentioned that we receive what is called a manifest. When you are the lead flight attendant, you always receive a manifest to let you know about any special people you may have onboard. No, I don't mean celebrities. The manifest usually contains the names of passengers with disabilities, passengers with pets, unaccompanied minors, any peanut allergies, and any armed individuals. Passengers with disabilities always pre board and I'm told about them by the operations agent. Sometimes, they show up later during boarding, and I am not made aware of who they are or where they are sitting, as was the case in this next story.

I was perusing my manifest and noticed we were going to have a passenger who was hearing-impaired. We were done with the pre boards and I hadn't seen the hearing-impaired passenger, so I assumed they slipped by me or they would board later in the flight.

Passengers who occupy the first row of seats cannot place their items on the floor in front of them. They can only stow their bags in the overhead bins. I always make a point to warn passengers in advance of this FAA mandated rule. On this flight, I noticed a lady with fuchsia colored hair sitting in the front row. She had her purse on the floor.

"Ma'am? Ma'am?" I said.

No answer. I leaned in close because I assumed that the reason she didn't respond was that she must have had ear buds in her ears.

"Ma'am? Hello?" I tried again. Nothing.

I waved my hand in her face.

A lady tapped me from behind. "I think she is deaf," she said.

Oh, I thought. I tapped Ms. Fuchsia on the shoulder and finally she looked at me. I pointed at her purse, shook my head no, pointed to her purse again and then at the overhead bin.

The lady rolled her neck and shook her head. "Argh," she said, snatching up her purse and placed it in her lap, rolling her eyes and turning to look out the window as if telling me our "conversation" was over.

I tapped her on the arm, gestured with both hands for her to rise, and then I pointed to the back of the plane.

She understood that, grabbed her purse, and walked away, but not before giving me one last eye/neck roll combo.

The silent exchange left me too exhausted to tell her that

you can't be deaf and ghetto. Pick a struggle.

SILENCING PORTABLE ELECTRONIC DEVICES

I hate that I have to ask you to silence your electronic devices.

You are free to do what you want in the privacy of your own vehicle, but when you are a guest in my vehicle, you need to be considerate. Do you really need to listen to the music as you obsessively play Candy Crush? Do you think people want to hear your child listen to Dora the Explorer? Nobody wants to hear the sex scene from the book that is currently turning you on, Sir. I hope you don't get a boner because then you are really going to piss me off.

When you are on my flight, I require that you use headphones and if you do not have any headphones, then you must turn your volume off. I do not care about your attitude, you are just one person out of the 100+ passengers that I am responsible for and it is not all about you. Sounds reasonable to me, but not to all of my passengers, like this lady.

"Excuse me ma'am, but could you please use your headphones?"

"I don't have any. Do you have some I can use?"

"I am sorry, we do not carry headphones. If you do not have any headphones, you must turn your volume down."

She huffed and puffed but did as asked and stowed her device.

I went back to my seat and within five minutes, I heard her game again.

"Ma'am, I am not going to ask you again to please turn your volume off."

This time, she turned to look out the window and ignore me.

I tapped the gentleman sitting next to her and the teenage boy on the aisle and asked them to remove their headphones and play their devices as loud as they wanted as Ms. I Won't Turn my Device Off looked on in horror.

Oh, now you are annoyed? Good, because we've all been annoyed with you, Ma'am. Enjoy the rest of the flight!

Chapter 14

Maybe I Should Write This S*** Down

After 9/11, we started offering heavily discounted rates and began attracting unsavory characters. I remember working a flight from Little Rock to Dallas when a man boarded carrying his belongings in a black trash bag. *Surely, his bag broke at the airport and that was his only option*, I thought.

Sadly, when I tactfully asked him about the trash bag, he said, "Nope. This is my luggage."

That was certainly a new one. I don't think I am being mean when I say that if you can afford a plane ticket, you can at least afford a cheap bag.

The airline industry suffered as a whole when this new crop of passengers began invading our sacred element. No longer did people dress up and look to flying as an adventure to cherish. These new passengers were traveling on a Burger King budget with diva demands, and they started to piss me off. I was slowly but surely changing my happy-go-lucky ways due, in part, to stories like the one I am about to tell you (that will probably leave you with your mouth hanging open).

At the beginning of this particular trip, I was in a great mood. I was in a relationship. I was healthy and happy. I woke up on the right side of the bed and all was well. Our first night, we overnighted in Las Vegas, and I had a blast hanging out with friends. The second night, I had plans in Los Angeles and was looking forward to another great overnight. And then, my last flight of the day happened. This flight was from Phoenix to Los Angeles. We had a good mix of business passengers and a few people like the ones I just described.

I was the lead flight attendant and offered my usual greetings to people as they boarded. "Hello! How are you?"

Sometimes we know right away when we're going to have a problem passenger. It's akin to when a cat's hair stands up on its back; we just sense some shit is about to occur. The problem on this particular flight was named Stephanie. Stephanie boarded my plane looking like a typical L.A. patron—all kinds of plastic (face and boobs), the standard Louis Vuitton luggage, and sporting an expensive, ginormous YSL bag, and Christian Louboutins. I was digging her because I can relate to fashion and I appreciate beauty. When you get right to it, I am not a hater. I am a congratulator. When I said hello to Stephanie, she just looked at me and turned back around. *Okay*, I thought, maybe she had on a hearing aid and I just hadn't noticed it. I said hello again, and this time Stephanie made a hand-swipe gesture as if I was the help. That pissed me off! Of course, Stephanie sat her pert ass in my section. Not sure if this was a good thing or a bad thing, I was determined that my interaction with her would be limited. After we did our demonstrations, because I was the lead flight attendant, I walked through the cabin to make sure everybody was in compliance and found Stephanie was still yakking away on her cell phone.

"Miss, I need you to turn off your cell phone, please," I said to her.

Stephanie held up a finger and mouthed the words, "In a minute."

I lifted a brow. "We're on an active taxiway and your phone should have been turned off ten minutes ago. I need you to turn off your cell phone now or we can go back to the gate and you can get off this flight."

Stephanie shot me a look that would have killed if I had been susceptible to that sort of thing. "Fine! I'll turn it off."

I walked away, and heard her say, "Bitch!"

Really, that's how she wants to play this? *Okay, sure*, I thought.

During the beverage service, Stephanie ordered several drinks including a cranberry juice. I had to remind her on several occasions to remove her foot from the aisle so she didn't trip someone. When I realized that was her exact intention, I did just that . . . I tripped right over her foot, carrying her cranberry juice on my tray. Hehehe.

Stephanie shrieked. "Oh my God! You just spilled cranberry juice all over my white suit and it's ruined! How could you be so careless?"

"Oh, Ma'am, I am so sorry!" I said, wearing a look of

fake shock on my face. "I knew someone would trip over your foot in the aisle! Let me get you some paper towels."

Stephanie looked at me with a knowing gleam in her eyes, realizing she'd picked the wrong bitch to fuck with.

As I slowly walked away to get her some paper towels, I grinned as wide as a Cheshire cat.

It's on, you mother*&^%ers, I thought, and that's when I started writing it all down.

Chapter 15

Dear Diary,

Do. Not. Touch. Me.

attack (verb) \ə'tak\

: To set upon in a forceful, violent, hostile, or aggressive way, with or without a weapon.

You may think I am being extreme, but I promise you that if you do not learn to keep your hands off us, you are going to come across the wrong flight attendant and get seriously hurt. If, at any time, we feel our lives are in danger, you touch us inappropriately, or you fail to comply with the procedures onboard the aircraft, we can and will contact the authorities. You will be fined by the FAA for interrupting flight attendant duties and, depending on how aggressive you were, you could possibly go to jail. You probably did not know that most airports have a jail located on their property, did you? I would strongly advise you to reconsider your actions before you spend years regretting your hasty decision.

Shortly after starting my career, I was working a flight from Salt Lake City, when this twitchy 6'3" male passenger boarded the plane. I was concerned because he was traveling alone. Neither of the agents had any information on him. We decided to go despite our concern because some people just have that crazy look about them even when they are totally sane. About halfway through our flight, Mr. Twitchy entered the restroom located in the back of the plane near the galley. When he exited, he just stood in the galley. I was in the back with Tiffany, one of my crewmembers and he was making us quite nervous. The other flight attendant, Kelly, was in the forward portion of the plane and was not aware of what was going on.

We have a phone located in both galleys to call the pilots and we decided it was best to make the call from the front of the plane where Mr. Twitchy would not hear it. We figured that if he heard us talking in code, he would suspect something was up and we did not want to set him off. I walked to the front of the plane and called the pilots. They asked me to keep them updated and, in the meantime, they would contact the authorities and keep them abreast of the situation.

When Kelly and I went to the back to check on Tiffany, we found her pinned in the corner by the odd passenger who would not let her go. Her eyes were wide and frightened. She talked calmly to placate him while we took action. We could not call the pilots because he was blocking the phone so Kelly and I screamed for help. Two male passengers came to our rescue. We made passengers from the last row move so that we could detain the crazy passenger until landing. We placed Mr. Twitchy in flex ties and the two male passengers who'd come to our rescue sat with him while we contacted the pilot. The passenger started rocking back and forth and muttering strange things.

As a crew, we made the decision to divert the plane to another city so we could have the passenger removed. I made the announcement for everyone to remain seated once we landed so that we could have the crazy passenger escorted off the plane. When we arrived at the gate, he sprinted through the cabin as soon as he was freed, running out the front door, and right into the arms of six burly policemen who were waiting for him in the jetway. He tried to resist and they threw him down on the ground and handcuffed him.

We were quite shaken up after the incident and found out later that he was actually a mental patient who had just been released from a facility. We were required by our company to write a detailed letter about the incident, but it never went to trial, so we never had to testify and we did not learn anything else about what happened to him.

Please be advised that if you are so unruly that your antics interrupt a flight, you can be assured that you are going to jail in whatever city we divert to and you will be on your own as far as getting transportation back home. It is equally against the law for you to get into a physical altercation with anyone else onboard an aircraft so behave yourself and keep your crazy at home.

FISTS OF FURY

We were flying from Las Vegas and I was the flight attendant working in the back part of the aircraft. During boarding, I was having a conversation with the other flight attendant when we noticed this couple coming to the back of the plane was cussing each other out. We stopped chatting and began to listen to the drama.

The woman sat in the last row of seats in the middle seat and the man sat in the row in front of her, also in the middle seat. As we stood there, we witnessed them arguing back and forth with the occasional "bitch" and "cunt" being thrown between them. I was just about to approach them regarding their language when the male turned around and punched the woman square in the face! I could not believe what I had just witnessed and my mouth actually fell open in disbelief. The woman was so embarrassed that she just sat there and did not say a word. The man began taunting her and that was it . . . I'd had enough. I told him that what he had done was unacceptable and that I was going to call the authorities. I asked her if she was okay and if she needed anything, and she said no. The police came and escorted both of them off the flight. Maybe they had never heard the slogan, "What happens in Vegas, stays in Vegas".

DO. NOT. POKE. ME.

poke (verb) \ pōk\
: To push, especially with something narrow or pointed, as a finger, elbow, stick, etc.

When you boarded my flight, did you happen to notice that I was not wearing a hearing aid? Then why did you just poke me to get my attention? I am not deaf and I assure you that a simple, "Excuse me", "Miss", "Ma'am" (hell, even

"Stewardess") would be preferable to you poking me.

I detest when strangers touch me, and when they do, I view it as an invitation to poke them back.

Poke!

"What do you want?" I asked, poking the passenger back.

"Ouch, you poked me!"

"You poked me first! Please Do. Not. Touch. Me. I can hear you just fine. What can be so important that you had to poke me?"

The poking passenger pouted, looking offended and a tiny bit hurt. "I didn't want anything."

I don't give a damn that her feelings were hurt! I am not a pony in a petting zoo. Let me please remind you that when you purchased your ticket, you purchased access to me verbally not physically. You do not have the right to touch me for any reason unless you're gently tapping my shoulder to tell me how pretty you think I am or pushing me clear of certain danger. Only under those circumstances is it okay for you to touch me.

DO. NOT. TOUCH. MY. BUTT

I know when I walk by you my butt just happens to be an arm's length away, but I would strongly advise you not to touch it to get my attention. I have crazy reflexes and they may cause me to slap you.

Once, I was standing in the aisle addressing a passenger when I felt a caress over my right butt cheek. WTF?! When I looked at the passenger responsible for the caress, he gave me what he must have thought was his sexy look and told me he wanted to order a vodka tonic.

I bent way down, gave him my sexy look, pinched him on his arm, and said, "Sir, I will spike your vodka tonic with Visine if you even think of getting near my ass again. Are we clear?"

He nodded. "Crystal." Then he changed his mind and no longer wanted a vodka tonic after all.

We do have traffic jams in the aisle and because they are narrow, it can be difficult trying to maneuver by some people. On another flight, I was about to proceed down the aisle when at the same time, this rather wide woman was approaching me. To let me pass, she turned towards the passenger sitting on the aisle, therefore putting her extreme girth in his face (uncomfortable). I just looked at her, shook my head and kindly gave her the right of way because there was no way I could get by her. That is the appropriate way to maneuver by someone in the aisle.

To the gentleman I just elbowed in the balls: I know you saw me coming down the aisle and figured this would be your lucky day to cop a feel of a flight attendant. Instead of being courteous and turning your "junk" into the face (so sorry) of the passenger sitting on the aisle seat, you turned toward me and because the aisles are narrow, as we passed each other, I felt your "junk" graze my butt. Because you could not tell how pissed I was, I just thought I would show you. And that is why toward the end of your free graze I "accidentally" elbowed you in the nuts. While you were bending over in pain and I was apologizing, you did not happen to notice that I was not sorry at all. I was just following protocol. Bet you won't try that one again, will you?

Chapter 16

Dear Diary,

Just don't . . .

O ver the years, I have developed a myriad of pet peeves, but my #1 pet peeve of all time is when you have the audacity to tell me to "SMILE". I am 99.9% sure that we do not know each other, so I would like to know who or what gave you the right to tell me to smile? I really want to go off with expletives even just telling you about it, but I will try my best to contain my anger.

How Dare You?!

You have no idea how my morning has gone. I may have had a car accident on my way to work. Maybe I had a flat tire. Maybe I got into an argument with my boyfriend and, because I have to be cooped up with you for the next three hours, we cannot resolve our problems, leaving me with no closure. I am sorry that I don't have a fake smile plastered on my face at all times. Maybe you forgot that I am a damned flight attendant and not a Dallas Cowboys cheerleader. Did it ever occur to you that absolutely nothing is wrong with me? Maybe I don't feel like grinning at 5:00 AM because I am f-ing tired!

Whatever my reason, you need to shut up, take a seat, and be happy my tired ass showed up to work so you can get to your destination. How about the next time I visit your office, I make a point to tell you to smile, and see how that makes you feel?

Usually, nothing is wrong with me. My mind is preoccupied with my life outside of work, and because I am very good at multitasking, I can greet you like a robot while reminiscing over the wonderful time I had last night.

I Hate to Bother You

Then why are you? I really, really hate when passengers say this. If they really hated to bother me, then they would not bother me (and I would not have to share this peeve with you).

On a recent flight, I had just walked through the cabin to see if anyone needed anything else. Everyone seemed satisfied, so I got comfortable on my jumpseat and started digging into my salad.

One of the passengers found me, kneeled down so her face was level with mine (as if I was a five-year old) and said, "I really hate to bother you, but can I get a Coke?"

I really wanted to say, "Heifer, I just asked your ass if you wanted something five minutes ago." Instead, I said, "As soon as I have a chance I will get you a Coke."

"Oh, it's no rush, whenever you have time," she said, standing there for a bit longer as if she thought I was really going to stop enjoying my salad to get her a Coke.

I said I'd get her Coke when I had a chance and right then was not the time. When she realized that I was not budging, she went back to her seat. Five minutes went by and then she rang her call button. I looked up and realized it was her and I went back to eating my salad. When I finished, ten minutes later, I innocently inquired about the call button. Waiting was what she deserved for being so rude. There were other flight attendants onboard and when she saw that I was trying to enjoy my lunch, she should have made her way to the back of the plane to ask the other two for assistance (thereby proving to me that she really didn't mean to bother me).

You Look Sleepy

I woke up feeling as if I'd had an adequate amount of sleep. My hair was a work of art and my makeup was just amazing. To be honest, I was looking damned good and I had never felt more ready to begin greeting my passengers at 5:00 AM. The morning was going well and pleasantries and compliments galore were coming my way until he came onboard, with a line I suspected he'd been rehearsing the ten minutes he stood in the jetway.

"Good morning!" I said.

Looking me up and down, the man proclaimed, "You look sleepy."

"And you look old." Yes, I really did say that because I cannot believe he had the audacity to tell me that I looked sleepy. Talk about rude! But hey, thanks to the look on his face, I laughed so hard I almost peed my pants so thanks, Pal, the joke is on you!

MAKE JOKES ABOUT THE PILOTS

I love watching the news, but we all know the media loves nothing more than to sensationalize stories involving the airline industry. The last thing we need is for yahoos to come onboard and continue the onslaught.

After watching replays on the news about the two British pilots who fell asleep while their plane was on autopilot, I am sure the guy in the next story could not wait to deliver his line.

"Good morning, how are you?" I said as a man boarded.

"I am fine. Have the pilots had enough rest?" he stopped to ask.

"Of course they have."

"Oh good, because I was concerned." He laughed.

I let him slide as the news was fresh and I know some people cannot contain themselves. However, by day two, I'd had enough of the wisecracks.

"Good morning, how are you?" I greeted an oncoming passenger.

After moving his dentures into place, he asked, "Are the pilots awake in there?"

I glanced to the closed cockpit door, and answered in a lowered voice. "As a matter of fact, they are taking a nap. Any more questions?"

The passenger's eyebrows flew up and his mouth dropped

open. He was clearly appalled that I would say such a thing.

By then, I'd smiled and turned my attention elsewhere, dismissing his silly self and his silly question. I really don't know what he expected me to say, but he should be smart enough at his age to know that the joke is old and keeping it up only aggravates me.

APPROACH US AT THE AIRPORT

Flight attendants are paid from the time the aircraft door closes until it opens at the next stop. In between flights, when we are cleaning or trying to catch a five-minute break before the next group of passengers board (and you ask us for something to drink), we are not being paid.

The same goes when you see us sitting around in the airport trying to catch up on some phone calls, taking a nap, or grabbing a bite to eat; we are not being paid. In other words, we are not paid to communicate with you on our downtime, and guess what? We don't want to talk to you!

Once, I was sitting down and minding my own business, trying to make some phone calls, when a man came and sat by me.

"Hiya!" he said, "I see you work for Sun Airways. By any chance, do you know Doug McCarthy? He's a friend of mine from high school and he's been a pilot for you guys for about ten years. He is based in New York. Where are you based? How long have you been a flight attendant?"

I looked at him wearing my highly annoyed face, but to my chagrin, the look was lost on him. "No, I don't know him and I am not based in New York." I looked away, trying to go back to my phone calls, but he started waxing on about the first time he'd flown with us, telling me how much he loved us, and saying that he'd never fly another airline.

While all of that was great, he took up ten minutes of the thirty-minute break I had and forced me to excuse myself from my comfy spot to go and try to find a quiet corner far away from him and people like him who just don't have any respect for a person's break time.

INVADE OUR PERSONAL SPACE

Personal space is the region surrounding a person that they regard as psychologically theirs. Let me break it down to you in layman's terms.

Psychologists define personal space requirements as follows:

Intimate Distance = Six to eighteen inches. This level of physical distance often indicates a closer relationship or greater comfort between individuals.

Personal Distance = One and a half to four feet. Physical distance at this level usually occurs between people who are family members or close friends.

Social Distance = Four feet to twelve feet. This level of physical distance is often used with acquaintances you do not know well (such as a postal delivery worker you only see once a month). Here, a distance of ten to twelve feet may feel the most comfortable.

Read the definition of Social Distance again, because this is the category where you fall. I understand the metal

JUST DON'T . . .

tube we are trapped in together does not provide a lot of wiggle room, but because our personal space is very limited, I would really appreciate it if you would use some common sense and only invade mine if necessary. I cherish my personal space, and I get really anxious and uncomfortable when I am minding my own business and I turn around and you are right there in my face almost nose to nose.

The last time this happened, I said, "I beg your pardon, Sir?"

"I just wanted another glass of water," the passenger said, close enough for me to smell his old man's breath mixed with coffee.

I winced at the stench and backed up about four feet. "As soon as I finish providing everybody else with their first round of drinks, I will be more than happy to get you a refill." I smiled at him and glanced down the aisle to convey to him that he needed to go and sit down.

I didn't say what I was thinking which was, "Please don't stand there waiting as if I am going to stop what I am doing to assist you. In the meantime, a piece of gum would be much obliged. Thank you."

I get really uncomfortable when I am sitting on my jumpseat, minding my own business, and someone kneels down and gets in my face. That is totally uncalled for and just puts me in a very foul mood.

"I just wanted to know if I could have another snack," the last person who did this said.

"Ma'am, there is no need to get in my face, I can hear you just fine." I wished I'd eaten a ton of garlic.

Here's a hint . . . common sense is available to everyone free of charge (and who doesn't like getting things that are "free"?).

GO SHOELESS IN THE LAVATORY

I am getting hives just thinking about how disgusting some people are. As I mentioned earlier, the lavatories onboard are just glorified port-a-potties. Would you use the port-a-potty at a park barefoot? No? Then please don't do it on an airplane either.

I know you might naively think that wetness on the floor is just water, but no, silly, it is urine. Yes, good old piss from the man who can't aim straight, or from the little kid who wet his pants, or from a woman who squatted and didn't wipe the toilet seat. You're an adult, so flight attendants don't feel the need to warn you, but sometimes we take pity on people.

Seeing a passenger about to go into the restroom wearing socks but no shoes, I said, "Ma'am, if I were you, I would go back and put shoes on."

"Oh, it's okay. I'm wearing socks," she said, as if I couldn't see that for myself.

"Well, be my guest then. You are going to end up with urine on your socks."

"Are you serious?" She looked at me as if I was crazy.

Yes, we are very serious, you idiot, I thought. We know who goes in there and what goes on in there and when we give you advice, you should trust us. If I don't like you, I will just watch you stuff your wet, nasty socks back into your shoes and laugh under my breath (see, there's another reason to be nice to your flight attendants).

After reading this, I really hope you still don't think it is cool to tell people you have joined the "Mile High Club", because it's not as prestigious as you thought, getting it on in a urine-soaked porta-potty. It is actually quite disgusting, and just shows how nasty and low class some of you really are.

Years ago, we had disease-ridden pillows and blankets that we offered to passengers who were too cheap to buy their own set. I was working a late night, empty flight. We turned down all of the lights and after passing out pillows and blankets, we sat down in the cabin preparing to take our own naps. After about twenty minutes, I got up to use the restroom and decided that I might as well pick up trash since I was already up. As I was walking through the cabin, I noticed a man by the window with his head back resting on the seatback. He had a blanket spread over him and the two seats next to him. I had just made out the outline of a body under the blanket when I noticed it moving up and down near his crotch. WTF?!

Reaching out, I tapped the moving blanket. "Excuse me!"

There was no response and the movement continued, like the bobbing of a head.

I poked the moving blanket again, harder. "Excuse me! What do you think you are doing?"

Out from under the blanket came a female's head. "We were just having fun. You know, trying to join the "mile-high" club?"

Oh hell no, I thought, turning the lights on full blast and making an announcement. "I am very sorry, folks, but due to a couple of unsavory characters, the lights will have to remain on for the duration of the flight."

The couple was pissed, but I didn't care. "I can and will have you arrested for public indecency," I told them. Then, I made her move to another row and I went back to reading my book. I felt sorry the other passengers had to endure the bright lights for the last two hours of the flight, but don't look at me. It wasn't my fault!

Later as the couple was deplaning, I asked the man if he'd "finished", to which he gave me the finger (I took that as a no). Ha ha ha!

HEY, ALCOHOLIC?

As I said before, I really do try my best not to be so judgmental. Sometimes I can fake it verbally, but my facial expressions always give me away. If you want to know how I really feel, just look at my face, because it never lies.

I am an early riser and view my mornings as a sacred time to consume coffee, water, or some variety of juice, but definitely not any alcoholic beverages. Therefore, you can imagine my facial reaction (and stomach churning) at the thought of mixing an alcoholic beverage for someone at the sacred hour of 5:00 AM.

"Sir, can I get you anything to drink?" I asked.

"Yeah, I would like a bloody mary!" the passenger said,

rather loudly. Maybe he'd been drinking even before boarding the plane, though the very thought seemed insane to me.

"Excuse me, did you say a bloody mary?" I made a show of looking at my watch and giving him that look I am infamous for.

He laughed. "It's happy hour somewhere!"

"Actually, Sir, there is not a single city in the United States where they celebrate happy hour at 5:00 AM. There may be several countries where it might be happy hour when it's 5:00 AM in the U.S., but I am positive that you don't know them. So stop embarrassing yourself and know that everyone around you is judging you, shaking their heads at your obvious stupidity, and silently calling you an alcoholic. Also, please know that if you were my boyfriend this would be a deal breaker is what I really wanted to say.

TEXAS

The great state of Texas will always hold a special place in my heart. I have come to adore southerners with their charm and southern twangs. However, though people from Texas feel as if Texas is God's country, not everyone shares their sentiments. It is time that Texans understand that the word "coke" means just that . . . "Coke" and nothing else when you are using it to refer to a beverage.

"Ma'am, can I get you anything to drink?" I asked the lady on a flight from Dallas.

"Yes, I would like a Coke please."

I returned with the Coke she ordered and handed it to her.

Looking at me as if I had sprouted two heads, she said. "What's this? I said I wanted a Dr. Pepper."

"I'm sorry, but you ordered a Coke."

"In Texas, a Coke means a lot of things," she answered, as if that made perfect sense.

The last time I checked, a Coke was a Coke and a Dr. Pepper was a Dr. Pepper. Maybe that should be included in the lesson plan in school. Not only was she confused, but she thoroughly confused me too. I am still shaking my head over it, five years later.

And you call yourselves God's country.

IMITATE A CAN

A can is an aluminum cylinder filled with liquid. We serve drinks in cans to passengers every day. I am always confused when someone feels the need to demonstrate what a can looks like.

"Sir, can I get you anything to drink?"

"Can I get a can of Sprite?" the passenger replied, holding up his hands, and imitating the shape of a can to illustrate.

Why do people do this? Lately, it seems as if people take simple words and feel the need to explain them with hand gestures.

Just last week I encountered a lady who said she felt faint. I understood perfectly how she felt and I did not need her to go a step further by putting her hand on her head and then on her neck. What the heck did that have to do with feeling faint?

Yesterday, I asked a passenger if he wanted something to drink. He put his hand to his mouth and imitated drinking from a cup with his pinky finger sticking up. If you want something to drink, just say so. Hand gestures are totally unnecessary.

I understand this might seem like a petty thing to complain about, but it is just another thing on our list of things people do to aggravate us. I really should thank those of you who do this because I now know what the shape of a can looks like. I know how to tell from hand gestures that you feel faint and I also know from hand signals when you are thirsty.

EXPLANATIONS

Over the past several years, due to the phenomenon we know as reality television, Americans have developed a "TMI" (too much information) problem.

I particularly have issues with reality television because it has caused some of you to feel as if you need to share your personal problems with me. I am not Dr. Phil, so I really don't care. I do not care that you need water to soak your dentures. I do not care that you just got your boobs done and the pressure of the plane is causing them to hurt. I do not care that your milk froze up and you are unable to breast-feed and need warm water to heat up your baby's bottle. I do not care that you need to stretch because you pulled a muscle in your groin. I do not care if you are "dying of thirst" (because I highly doubt you are going to die right now if you do not receive a glass of water). I do not care that you have to go to the bathroom constantly because you have a weak bladder. I do not care that you were just diagnosed with depression because life is just not fair to you, and I particularly do not care to hear stories about your mother because I don't know you or her.

If you need water, just ask for it, no explanation needed. If you need to go to the lavatory, and the seat belt sign is illuminated, by law, I cannot give you permission to leave your seat. But, come on. We're all adults here. Just do what you have to do if it's an emergency. Please keep your personal business to yourself and stop explaining to me that what you ate did not agree with you while holding onto your stomach. All you are doing when you over share is interrupting my reading time and annoying me. Word of advice . . . if I don't ask, I don't care and I don't want to know.

While some things do not need an explanation, others do. I would have really appreciated a heads up before I made a complete fool of myself in this next story.

Dwarf

I know, the title already has some of you in a tizzy, but slow down and let me explain.

About seven years ago, I was the lead flight attendant and watched as a 6'5" man boarded my flight. Behind him, I briefly caught a glimpse of a wheelchair, but I had to go to the lavatory so did not see who it belonged to. When I exited the lavatory, the tall gentleman called me over to his seat and asked for a seat belt extension. I was confused because he looked very fit and didn't appear to need one. As I turned to get his seat belt extension, someone touched my leg. I looked down and saw the top of what I thought was a child's head. I wasn't in the mood to babysit anyone's child, but before I could inquire who she belonged to, she took the seat next to the tall guy.

After we finished boarding, I began to walk through the cabin to make sure that everyone was in compliance with all the rules so we could take off. As I approached the tall man and his child, I saw the child was standing on the seat.

"Sir, you are going to have to put your child in a seat and fasten her seat belt please."

"Miss, this is not my child. This is my wife!" he exclaimed.

When I looked closer, I realized I'd mistaken a grown-ass dwarf woman with clubfeet for a kid! I was mortified by what I had said and swiftly apologized.

That is when I saw what the seat belt extension was for—she was too short to sit in the seat, so she had to lean on a makeshift car seat with the seat belt extension wrapped around her and the car seat. She stood like that for the entire four-hour flight.

I don't know if I was more weirded out by her and her seat belt contraption or by the fact that she was the same height as a doll and was married to a giant! The other flight attendants and I did a lot of contemplating on this in the galley and came to the conclusion that there's a weird fetish out there for everyone.

FLASH GUT FLAB

Stowing your luggage in the overhead bin can be trying sometimes, especially if you have an oversized bag. Please know that we do not feel sorry for you when you stuff your bag so full that it is barely manageable and then come aboard our aircraft and break our overhead bins when you try to shove your big-ass bag into a space clearly too small for it.

While we do not feel sorry for you and your plight, we do feel sorry for the unlucky person seated on the aisle where you are standing. We cringe when we see you shoving your bags into the overhead bin, sweating buckets, and inadvertently placing your gut in the face of (and literally on the head of) the innocent passenger occupying the aisle seat. If you are one of the many Americans who have a shameless gut, it would behoove you to wear a top that is long enough to cover everything or be tucked into your pants. Thank you for your compliance (from the man whose bald head you just waxed with your hairy, sweating gut).

One more thing about gut flab . . . I am very aware of the latest trend in wearing half tops. Half tops are designed for women who have FLAT stomachs. A very small pooch is also accepted, but barely. If a small pooch is borderline acceptable, wearing a half top in public with a gut so large that you look pregnant is downright AWFUL. I am being very sincere and trying to help you when I tell you that I just noticed the set of guys staring at you with disgust written all over their faces. I also noticed the child who wanted to ask you if you were having a boy or a girl before their mother shut them up. I'm just sayin' that all trends are not made for everyone.

ORDER SPECIALTY ITEMS

Before the boom known as Starbucks took hold of this country, ordering coffee was simple. You either ordered it black, or asked for cream and/or sugar. Now, you can order your coffee non-fat, skinny, with soy milk, almond milk, goat's milk, and with whipped cream and sprinkles on top. You even have your choice of flavored coffees—bold, blonde, dark, etc. Even though you have a plethora of options at the coffee house, on airplanes we don't get that fancy. Some of you just don't understand this.

"Ma'am, can I get you something to drink?" I asked a passenger on a recent flight.

"I would like a cappuccino."

I laughed. "That's funny. But seriously, how would you like your coffee? Black? Cream and sugar?"

Let's keep it real L.A.—we both know you know better. How much did you pay for your ticket again? To be fair, residents of the east coast are also confused by my profession.

"Hi, Sir. Can I get you something to drink?"

"Yes, a coffee regular," the passenger said as if I am supposed to know what a coffee "regular" is.

I lifted a brow. "I beg your pardon? What is a coffee

141

regular?"

Recently, I learned that it is a coffee with cream and sugar. But, let me remind you that though I may look like your local Barista to some of you, I am not her. I am a flight attendant on an airplane that serves above average coffee with a lack of a selection. And that goes for tea too! We just have the basics, people. Just the basics.

While we are on the subject of ordering coffee, please keep in mind, that when I ask you a question it requires an actual answer.

"Sir, can I get you anything to drink?" I asked.

"I would like a coffee."

"Black, or cream and sugar?"

"Yes."

"I beg your pardon? Black or cream and sugar?" I repeated in case he didn't hear me the first time.

Here's another bit of advice for you when you travel. Get your head out of the darned *Wall Street Journal*, put your phone down, and pay attention when someone asks you a question. I don't like wasting my breath or my time, and I really get annoyed when (after having covered this with one person) the idiot sitting next to them does the same thing! Snap out of it, people!

About twelve years ago, I was working a flight from Dallas to Austin about 6:00 in the morning. The flight had sixty passengers onboard, so it was fairly open. Everyone was reading their newspapers and going over notes for upcoming business meetings, and it was very quiet. I walked through the cabin offering orange juice and coffee and encountered one of the best lines ever.

"Sir, would you like an orange juice or a coffee?"

"I would like some coffee, please."

"Would you like that black or with cream and sugar?"

"I would like my coffee black, like I like my women."

Holy crap! I almost dropped my tray. He could not tell I was blushing, but if I was white, he would have seen that my cheeks were beet red. Thank goodness, it was also dark in the cabin because I also broke out in a sweat from being put on the spot like that. Everyone within five rows began peering around their newspapers, and a few cleared their throats. Then it became eerily silent. I shakily handed him his coffee, thanked him, and then asked him to come to the back galley. I did not want to speak to him in front of the other passengers, who still looked at us wearing expectant expressions (so sorry I let you down). As soon as I finished my service, I ran to the galley and told the other flight attendants what had happened. They both grabbed trash bags as an excuse to walk through the cabin to check him out. Eventually, he came to the back and I found out his name was David. He was very nice and extremely hot, but I had a boyfriend and had to let David down gently. He understood and did not pull a douche move by insisting I take his business card, "just in case". I ended our exchange with a lot of respect for him.

HOT CHOCOLATE

Nothing gets a flight attendant's panties in a twist more than when someone orders hot chocolate. I do not understand why we hate this powdered mixture so much, but order one and watch how our attitude changes.

One day, I was in a rhythm taking drink orders. Passengers were ordering Coke, Sprite, and water. Some even ordered two drinks, but then I came to the man who messed up my rhythm.

"Sir, can I get you anything to drink?"

"Can I get a hot chocolate?" the very adult, tall passenger said.

I gave him the look of death and waited to see if he was just kidding. After a second, I realized he wasn't joking. Hot under the collar, I went to the back galley and told the other flight attendant about the grown man who'd ordered hot chocolate. She became equally pissed off because men should never, ever even think about ordering a hot chocolate. It's just not a manly thing to ask for.

Several years back, an unaccompanied minor on my flight ordered hot chocolate. When I brought it to him, I put a lid on it and added some ice cubes to his cup so it wouldn't be too hot.

"Oh man!" he said when I gave it to him.

"What's wrong?"

"My mom told me to order hot chocolate and to spill it on myself," he answered.

The length some of you will go to in order to earn a quick buck never fails to amaze me. Unfortunately, for that kid's mom, I had the authorities and child protective services called. I hope that conniving mom learned her lesson.

Seriously, the hot chocolate thing has to stop. We hate opening the packets and watching the powder fly everywhere. It's just so messy. Having to mix it for you really irks us. We especially hate when you order one for your child because all they are going to do is make a big mess that most of you will just leave for us to clean up. You have obviously confused me for your housekeeper (not!). Just so we are clear, we hate it when you order hot chocolate and we hate you too.

The same thing goes for iced tea. If my airline wanted to sell iced tea, then it would be an option. But it is not an option. Why don't you look at our in-flight menu if you think I am lying to you? Yes, we have tea and we have ice, but we do not have iced tea. However, I will bring you what you need so you can make your own damned iced tea.

No, we do not have lemonade either. Yes, we have lemons, water, and sugar, but lemonade is not an option on our menu. You want to make some lemonade? Knock yourself out. Just don't you dare ask for something I am not offering!

"Ma'am, would you like some peanuts?"

"Pretzels."

I'm sorry, maybe you misunderstood me, but I did not offer you any pretzels.

"Sir, would you like some peanuts?"

"Do you have any cookies or crackers? They did on the last flight."

"Well, on this flight we are offering peanuts, but they do

have cookies and crackers in the airport."

You should be happy we are even offering you a free snack! Some people can be so rude and ungrateful.

SIT IN THE LAST ROW OF SEATS

We always know in advance how booked our flights are and we relish the opportunity to sit in a "real" seat when we know a flight is lightly booked. We usually put our bags on the last row of seats to hold them and make it obvious that you are not welcome to sit there. We even go as far as directing you to other seats so you stay as far away from us as possible.

When you see that everybody has occupied seats in the front of the aircraft, why do you ignore the obvious hints and sit your ass back here annoying us? Don't tell me you didn't notice that we are highly irritated with you. You didn't notice the look of death I gave you when you smiled that goofy smile and said, "It's nice back here, all by myself." You didn't take the hint when I didn't smile or respond to you? You didn't notice that when the other flight attendant came to the back, she pointedly looked at you and then looked at me and raised her hands in a questioning gesture as if she was asking, "Why in the hell is he sitting back here?" Again, pay attention people!

We run into some passengers who have absolutely no life. Their only entertainment is to listen to the flight attendants gossiping about their drama-filled lives. Those are usually the ones who clamor for the last row of seats, sit on the aisle, and constantly look back at us as if we are going to invite them into our conversations (which we will not do). Because you are sitting back here, irritating us, we will irritate you and be as loud as possible. We will slam the compartments in our galley, congregate in the aisle, and share stories with each other, cackling as loudly as we can. Oh, were you trying to take a nap? Sorry! You might want to move your ass to the front of the aircraft if you want to take a nap on this three-hour flight because if you continue to sit back here, it's going to be a long one.

The following is dedicated to you, my fellow crewmembers.

Chapter 17

Dear Diary,

Why am I flying with this crazy-ass flight attendant?

There are so many things I love about my job, and one of them is having the ability to fly with friends.

Every month, we "bid" for our schedule for the following month. Bid lines show availability for one-day trips (turns), two-day trips, three-day trips, and four-day trips. Each pairing (trip) lists the overnight, length of the overnight, your report times, and how many flights you will fly for the duration of the trip. Every airline has different ways of bidding, but regardless, seniority is the name of the game.

At my airline, if I want to fly with two of my friends, then we will all bid the exact same lines. If we are around the same seniority then our chances of being awarded the same line is good. Because of my seniority, I typically work Monday through Wednesday. Some friends I adore, with low seniority, have to work on the weekends sometimes, but I refuse to work weekends. When our lines are awarded, we have the option to trade with each other and we can also trade unawarded trips with the company.

We trade for all sorts of reasons—for certain days off, to

extend a vacation, or to fly with friends (just to name a few). With so many options, we can almost always fly with someone we know. However, we do fly with people we are not familiar with and sometimes this can pose a problem or two.

The List

Every airline has several flight attendant bases. For a city to become a base, it usually has to be around the airline's headquarters and have a high volume of flights coming in and out of the airport. The more flights there are, the more attendants are needed.

At my airline, we have seven bases and every base has a "no-fly list". This list is composed of the names of flight attendants who are bullies, rude, consistently lazy, dirty, or have bad hygiene, bad attitudes, or who are whores, or just strange. Flight attendants all familiarize themselves with this list and sensitive types try to avoid flying with the offending characters. To get on the list, it takes more than a one-time incident. You have to be consistent in your behavior and your name must have floated down multiple gossip chains. If you make the list, you have a file as thick as my butt.

A file is what the company keeps on every flight attendant throughout their entire career. Within the files are good and bad letters received from customers and employees, medical leave and FMLA notes, and information about whether or not you belong to a substance abuse program. Your sick time and on the job injury complaints are in there as well as notes about meetings with management and any disciplinary action that was taken against you as well as assessments on your appearance in uniform. It is also a given that if your name is on the "list" the other positions on your trip will almost always be available because nobody wants to fly with you. As I mentioned earlier, seniority is the name of the game and if you happen to be at the low end of the totem pole, well, it sucks to be you.

I have flown out of four of our bases and have become loosely familiar with the "list" at each base. I say loosely because I am not nosey, I am not easily offended, and I usually keep to myself. Therefore, I do not have a problem with most people. As long as you do your job, perform your safety related duties, and stay out of my business, we will have a good trip together. That is not to say that people do not have a problem with me.

Over the years, comments about me have run the gamut. I usually hear that I am beautiful and fun to fly with or that I am crazy, but in a good way. I love it when fellow flight attendants tell me that after flying with me they were inspired to work out, to eat healthy, or to work extra trips to get out of debt. I also hear many people say that I am quiet and very abrupt. Which part of me you see depends a lot on who I am flying with.

Years ago, my girlfriend was on the hotel shuttle headed to her overnight. Another set of crewmembers joined her and her crew in the shuttle. As soon as they were settled, one of the other flight attendants asked my friend where she was based. When my friend replied that she was Texas based, the nosey flight attendant asked, "Do you know Sydney Pearl?"

My friend got the feeling that she was about to hear some gossip about me, so she lied and said, "No."

"Well, she's beautiful, but sometimes she can be so abrupt," the flight attendant said.

My friend was upset because she knows me personally. "Actually, Sydney is a very good friend of mine and either she likes you or she doesn't."

The flight attendant started stuttering and trying to apologize, but it was too late.

When I found out about the exchange later, I just laughed because it did not bother me. Sometimes, when you fly with people you don't get along with, it is just a matter of conflicting personalities. I also know that if we do not get along, chances are we may never fly together again.

I am not sure if I am on somebody's "list", and guess what? I don't give a damn either way.

SHUTTER ISLAND

We stereotype company bases like we stereotype people. Out of our seven bases, some have specific qualities that make them stand out from the pack. One of our bases is known for their "hard bodies", one for being "ghetto", one is named "Fairy Tale" (get it?), and one is named "Shutter Island".

The name Shutter Island is well deserved, as this is the base where most of the crazies go. They are not forced here like at an insane asylum. This base just happens to be a junior base. A junior base is usually full of flight attendants who have not been flying for very long, but they act as if they have been flying forever because their seniority is so good there. Let me explain it to you. See, if a flight attendant is based in one of our senior bases in Texas and the most senior flight attendant has been flying for fifty years (yes, your math is correct, she is over seventy years of age), and if the base only holds 600 flight attendants who have been flying for fifteen plus years and you are new with only one year under your belt, then you are at the bottom of the totem pole. Your seniority will hardly ever change because they have restricted the amount of flight attendants at that base. Hence, you will never really have any seniority. Now, if you transfer to Shutter Island and the most senior flight attendant has been there only five plus years, and that base can accommodate 1500 flight attendants, you will not be at the bottom of the seniority list because as the airline hires new employees, they will come to your base and be placed under you. Do you get it now? Good. Moving on.

Due to my living situation, I had to be based out of Shutter Island for a couple of years and I will tell you that the name is very appropriate for this west coast base. I told you earlier that I think the majority of crazy people come from the west coast, or maybe they move there and become crazy. At any rate, they are total nut jobs. As soon as I transferred to this base, I became familiar with the characters on the "list". One infamous character went by the name of "Birdman". Birdman got his name because when he was in the galley making drinks, he constantly put water on his hands from the coffee pot spigot and ran his fingers through the front of his hair (kind of like how a bird constantly dips their beak in water and then cleans their feathers). Birdman also took it a step further. While he was in the aisle, passing out drinks, he would sometimes dip his fingers in a passenger's cup, and then run them through his hair before handing the passenger their drink.

Another resident of Shutter Island was a flight attendant named Raymond. Raymond was a senior flight attendant, having flown for about fifteen years. I am not sure when Raymond went cuckoo, but he developed a behavioral disorder known as scatolia, better known as the smearing of one's own feces. In other words, Raymond liked to play with his own shit. When he would get to his room, he would have an "episode" and cover his room with feces. I was always the most disturbed by this character because nobody knew who he really was except our union representatives and they cannot divulge such information due to legalities. Fortunately, I heard recently that he now only flies day trips. Still, I am a germaphobe and I would shit my pants if I had to fly with him. No pun intended.

Rounding out the list of over-the-top patients on Shutter Island is Nancy, the random flasher. Nancy, like Raymond, is another senior flight attendant who went a little nuts later in life. I think it had something to do with finding her now ex-husband (who is still currently a pilot with Sun Airways) in bed with another man. I will get to that juicy tidbit a little later.

I happened to fly with Nancy and was shocked to find out later that her name was on the "list" because she did not exhibit any erratic behavior the entire time we flew together. My friend Phil was not so lucky. He had to endure her antics for three days. According to him, they were in the back galley when Nancy just randomly pulled out one of her boobs. She was literally using one hand to massage her boob while using her other hand to pour passengers' drinks! Phil was appalled and embarrassed at what he witnessed. Later, during the day, Nancy turned off the lights in the back galley, took her clothes off, and started streaking back and forth in the back of the plane. Phil called a supervisor who told him that they were aware of Nancy and her behavior. He told Phil to write a report so they could add it to her file. Case closed.

BAD HYGIENE

Within three months of my arrival on Shutter Island, I knew all about the list, but I hadn't met anyone on it. When I received my trip sheets and saw a new name listed as crew, I'd ask other flight attendants in the lounge if they were familiar with the person so I could get the scoop on them before our initial flight. One Monday morning, I checked in for a trip and saw two unfamiliar names listed on my trip sheet. I asked Heather, a flight attendant I had recently flown with, if she knew who they were. Heather told me she knew Angie and vouched for her, but she said she was unfamiliar with a junior flight attendant named Tamara.

I met my crew in the jetway before the start of our trip.

As I turned to speak to Tamara, I caught a whiff of a very foul smell. I didn't want to assume it was her or pass judgment after such a brief first encounter. When we sat on the jump-seats in preparation for takeoff, Tamara turned to me and said something I could not understand, and then she laughed. The foul odor that came from her mouth was so shocking it rendered me speechless. I did my best to give her sublim-inal signs that all conversation was off, leaning as far into the door as possible, giving non-committal grunts instead of actual replies, and turning my face forward, refusing to face her. But she never took the hint, and just kept on yakking.

I started my inflight service immediately on day two. Normally on a four-hour flight, we start service within twen-ty or thirty minutes after takeoff, but that day I started ten minutes after takeoff. Tamara caught the hint this time and stopped talking. On day three, I noticed her hair was ex-tremely greasy and that she had dandruff flakes on her shoul-ders. She scratched her head frequently, causing snowflakes to fall. I wanted to puke. When the trip was over, I created my own list and she was the number one offender. I talked about her to every single person I flew with afterwards.

Two months into my short stay on Shutter Island, I checked in for another three-day trip. I was vaguely familiar with the names on my trip sheet, so I was pretty psyched as I headed toward my plane. As I was chatting with Amy, an-other crewmember, I felt a tap on my shoulder.

It was Tamara. "Hey, Girl! I guess we're flying together again!" She grinned.

"Since when? Matthew is listed on my trip sheet."

Tamara shrugged. "He must have called in sick because scheduling called and told me this was my trip now."

Although she was happy as a clam, I was pissed as hell. I wanted to call karma and ask what in the hell I had done to deserve this. I caught a whiff of what I was sure was a rotten tooth, and my stomach began to get queasy. I called an inflight supervisor and complained about her hygiene. A supervisor named Michelle came to the plane under the pretense of giving all of us a uniform evaluation. Michelle could not pull Tamara from the trip because she was in full compliance, but she did tell Tamara to be mindful of the snowflakes on her uniform.

As soon as we took off, Tamara started talking as if she did not have a clue in the world that she stunk. She got on my last good nerve, and there was no way I was going to subject myself to another three days of torture.

This time around, I leaned away from her, slowly turned my head and said, "Oh my God, did you have garlic for breakfast?"

"No." She frowned and covered her mouth.

"Well, something smells like garlic and it STINKS!"

She did the palm test (that doesn't work) to check her breath when I got up from my jumpseat. It was kudos to me from the rest of the crew because for the remainder of the trip, not only did she keep her distance, but she also started getting up from her jumpseat within ten minutes after takeoff.

For the remainder of my stay at Shutter Island, I never saw her again, but I was armed with Altoids and mouthwash just in case.

NOSEY FLIGHT ATTENDANTS

Nosey flight attendants have no couth. They are sneaky little people, adept at making others feel as if they are interested in you when they are secretly comparing themselves to you and trying to figure out how to one-up you.

One of my most memorable moments occurred when I was based in Texas. I was working a trip with Jennifer, who looked like your typical Dallas woman—big, blonde hair extensions, big, fake boobs, veneers, and the obligatory fake laugh and seeming affection whilst secretly giving you the once-over.

I abhor fake people, so I was already in a mood that only grew when I realized that Jennifer's friendliness toward me stopped just short of greeting me.

While the rest of the crew received the smile full of veneers, I received a curt, "Hi, and you are?"

"I am Sydney," I replied, watching her slyly giving me the once-over, noticing everything—my perfectly styled extensions, my diamond earrings and manicured nails, ginormous engagement ring, tailored/dry cleaned uniform and Gucci pumps.

Jennifer didn't realize she was flying with a wildcat who would verbally claw her ass to death. It was clear that Jennifer was not used to someone upstaging her. I soon realized her phoniness stemmed from being an ex-cheerleader and a pageant contestant (but not an actual winner).

I knew she could not wait to get in my business, so I got the catnip ready. As soon as my butt touched the jumpseat, she turned to me, her posture aggressive.

"I've never seen you before," she said.

"Considering we have 8,000 flight attendants, I'm sure you haven't seen all of us."

"Where do you live?"

"Uptown."

"Oh my gawd, I love Uptown! It's like, only ten minutes from my house in Highland Park."

I smiled as she name dropped her neighborhood and didn't give her the satisfaction of acknowledging it.

"Your hair is gorgeous and so long," she said, giving me the once over again.

"Are you trying to insinuate something?"

She blushed, knowing she was being called out. "No, I was just sayin'."

I gave her the stink eye and turned away.

"Wow, check out your rock! What does your guy do?"

Turning back to her, I lifted a brow. "Apparently, something yours does not."

That shut her up. I knew I'd hurt her feelings, but I did not care. I slowly got up from the jumpseat and sauntered away to take my drink orders. For the rest of the trip, we sat in silence that was very comfortable for me, but very uncomfortable for her.

On the last day of the trip, as we were leaving the airplane, Jennifer turned to me with that megawatt fake smile and said, "It was so good flying with you!"

My response? Crickets.

I really do not know why flight attendants always feel the need to say, "It was great flying with you," when it wasn't. When we are off the clock, I am no longer paid to be cordial to you, and I will cease to do so if you deserve it. Do yourself a favor, I'd like to say, just gather your belongings and quietly leave the aircraft. If that's too hard for you, then get on your phone and pretend like you are on a call. Whatever you do, just stop being fake with everyone! And enough with the million questions about my personal business! How is knowing any of my business going to help you in your life?

A few months later, I happened to run into Jennifer on the hotel shuttle heading to the airport.

"Hey, Girl!" she exclaimed.

I rolled my eyes. "Jennifer, you know I don't like you."

A few crewmembers laughed until they realized I wasn't joking, and then it became awkwardly silent.

Oh well, I told you I hate fake people!

CHATTY CATHY

Chatty Cathys are obnoxious people (usually women). Chatty Cathys bother me so much because, with them, it's just endless chatter about absolutely nothing of importance. Silence makes them very uncomfortable and for this reason, they always feel the need to fill quiet with talking.

I like going to work on the early morning shift. On the shuttle to the airport, if it is still dark outside, it is nice to savor those last few precious moments to myself and maybe take a quick nap while riding in the nice, dark, and quiet van. I live in the Central Standard Time zone, but on this particular trip, I was working on the east coast. The night before, I hadn't gone to sleep until midnight. I finally managed to go to sleep, when my alarm jolted me awake at 3:30 AM Eastern Standard Time (2:30 AM Central Standard Time!). I was so disoriented that, for a moment, I forgot where I was. Somehow, I managed to get my bearings for my 4:30 AM lobby time. Lobby time is the time the crew needs to be on the hotel shuttle bound for the airport. This particular hotel was located in the downtown area and it was at least a thirty-minute drive to the airport. I was so pumped thinking about the extra shuteye I was about to receive. I thought it was just going to be my flight crew along for the ride, but then I found out there would be ten of us riding to the airport. I hastened to a window seat, laid my head against the window, and got all snug and cozy with my coat acting as a blanket. Then, I spotted a cheery looking middle-aged soccer mom who seemed to be going through a mid-life crisis and knew she was going to ruin my quiet time.

"Good Morning, everyone!" she greeted us.

I rolled my eyes and everybody else grunted, but she would not be deterred, and turned to the flight attendant next to her.

"So, where are you based?" she asked. "Where are you

flying today? What are you going to do on your overnight?" And on and on until we arrived at the airport.

I am sure I wasn't the only one who wanted to smack her for ruining our last little bit of quiet before the storm. She should have thanked her lucky stars that she was not flying with me because I would have shut her up the same way I had the last one just like her I'd encountered only the week before.

We had a 5:00 AM check-in at the airport and I just wasn't really in the mood for it. "It" meaning work, people, drama, talking and faking being nice. I ended up flying with some hippy little flight attendant who reminded me of an obnoxious lap dog. From the time we introduced ourselves in the lounge, she was yakking to any and everybody like she was the mayor or somebody just as important. I was growing more agitated by the minute at the sound of her high-pitched laugh and country accent. I hoped, for her sake, that by the time we actually got on the plane she would simmer down a bit, but no such luck. I gave her all kinds of subliminal hints that all conversation was off limits, but after fifteen minutes, she started fidgeting and I knew she was going to start in.

"So, what are your plans when we get to San Diego?" she asked.

I held up my hand. "It is too early for all of this chatting and I am not in the mood."

She looked like a wounded mutt on the verge of tears. But she shut the hell up and I had a great rest of the morning!

Chatty Cathys love "TMI". Within thirty minutes of

meeting one, I know their life story, about the lazy husband who has decided to let himself go, about the affair with a pilot, the venereal disease contracted from said pilot, and the medicine cabinet they carry around because of a million ailments. I do sympathize, but I don't know them and, from the sound of it, they are not someone I want to get to know. Since they've already shown me they have diarrhea of the mouth, and I cannot trust them, I lie to them about everything just to see if it gets around. You'd better stay on my good side because if you do not, I may be compelled to spill the beans on your personal life and yes, names will be included.

Once, I was in the lounge prepping for a trip when I saw this grungy looking flight attendant. I thought, *if I was a guy, I would never screw her*. She was dumpy looking with bad acne, a wide ass, and she was sporting a camel toe and Dr. Martens. So gross. I saw her wedding ring and chalked it up to "there's somebody for everybody". As I proceeded to my aircraft, wouldn't you know it . . . I was flying with Camel Toe!

It's like when we go through security and spot the passenger with the most drama, or the irate business passenger, or the mom traveling with four rotten kids. They almost always end up on our flight as if karma is kicking us in the mouth or something. Anyway, I wasn't sitting for five minutes before Camel Toe turned to me.

"My husband is going to meet us at the hotel when we get there. We're going to be working on making a baby."

"Ummm. Okay," I said, disgusted at the image of her having sex. I couldn't imagine what her husband must look like.

Why do some people feel they need to share such personal information with complete strangers?

WHAT'S UP, CRACKHEAD?

Every airline has some sort of substance/alcohol abuse program available to their employees because, let's keep it real, having to deal with the general public really puts some of us over the edge. If you are a frequent flyer, then you may have come into contact with a flight attendant who was doped up on something. Whether it's Xanax, Vicodin, Ecstasy, Oxycontin, Quaaludes . . . you name it. And you thought that last flight attendant with the shaky hands and the sweating brows was just nervous. Not!

The problem with being an addict and working for an airline is the random drug and alcohol tests. When I say random, I mean random. I have been flying for almost twenty years and in that time, I have been tested for drugs and alcohol four times. However, people who are part of the substance abuse program are tested much more often. Of course, supervisors maintain that the selection is perfectly random, but we are not stupid. We know better. It makes common sense that if an employee has a known problem, they should be "randomly" tested more. Could you imagine the repercussions if a passenger was injured by a flight attendant who'd been in and out of rehab and who was doped up at the time of the injury?

The only way around "random" drug tests is to have an inside connection. Years ago, we had a flight attendant by the name of Ted who was abusing prescription painkillers. Before his last flight back to his base, he called in sick, changed his clothes, donned a baseball cap, and flew home. He sat in the front row and as soon as the doors opened at the end of the flight, he took off running. Nobody knew who he was, as he was dressed as a regular passenger. Over the course of a year, the company tried to nail this guy down for drug testing. Somehow, Ted was always one step ahead of them. They figured out that he was being tipped off by someone in our scheduling department who also would book him on an overnight because drug and alcohol tests are always performed at the end of a trip once the flight attendant is back at their base. Flight attendants are never tested when they start their overnight unless they have a history of abuse.

One day, when Ted was working in the back of the plane and got the call that he was being tested, he took off his wings and tried to sneak onto the provisioning truck, apparently to make a run for it on the tarmac. But his nine lives had run out. They caught him and when he tested positive, he was fired when the company received his test results.

Once you test positive, there is no way for you to get your job back unless you have a compelling reason for being retested, and that test comes out negative. There have been flight attendants who have inadvertently tested positive because the prescription drugs they were on happened to contain trace amounts of whatever drugs they were being tested for, who were able to get their jobs back.

There are tons of flight attendants who have alcohol abuse problems. I have encountered one slumped in her jumpseat, drunk as a skunk and another who locked herself in the plane's bathroom to sleep off the alcohol. I have even seen flight attendants take a sip of a passenger's alcoholic beverage as they were mixing drinks in the back galley. Don't worry, they always used a straw as they just need a little "taste" to take the edge off.

Flying with a flight attendant who is doped up or drunk can be dangerous, especially if an emergency arises. My girlfriend, Venessa was flying with Tracy and did not know anything was amiss until they had a medical situation onboard. While performing CPR on a passenger, Tracy could not get her counts down or figure out the correct position for her hands. At first, Venessa thought she was just nervous until they had to perform rescue breathing on the passenger. When the passenger came to, she accused them of giving her Jack Daniels. Everybody was confused until the paramedics smelled the tube of the CPR mask and detected the smell of alcohol. Authorities were already on hand due to the emergency. The flight attendants were tested and like Ted, Tracy was gone soon afterwards.

WHEN ALCOHOL GOES BAD

About seven years ago, my friend Michelle was out drinking. Michelle was on call and could be called as early as 3:00

AM for a 5:00 AM report time. She was sure she would not be called and proceeded to party and get drunk until she was called into work. The alcohol had clearly clouded her thinking because she told them she was drunk and could not accept the assignment. Say what? Our company policy is that you cannot consume any alcoholic beverage eight hours prior to reporting to work. What an idiot! She should have just gone to work and played it off to her flight crew by claiming she had a stomach virus. Instead, after twelve years of flying, another one bites the dust.

The problem with alcohol is that most pilots and flight attendants head to the bar when they arrive for their overnight, and it only takes a little too much alcohol to make them do and say stupid things that they will regret the next day. For this reason, I usually decline to hang out with crews in bars. I always mentally count until someone brings up what I like to call "forbidden topics"—sex, religion, and race. The minute the conversation delves into these regions, it usually ends up making someone very uncomfortable and I would rather not be involved.

I especially had a hard time dealing with some of our pilots during the presidential race leading up to President Obama's first term in office. I find it interesting how the typical white pilot is cool to fly with, but as soon as he gets a little liquor in him, his true colors come out.

One night, I was all for slam clicking on my crew, but we'd had such a great day flying together that I decided to hang out for a bit. Everything was fine until we saw on the news that President Obama had just won the election.

The pilot said, "He only won because of the minority and gay vote."

Everyone was silent and I wanted to scratch his eyes out, but instead, I said, "Minorities and gays are not the only people who voted for him. You didn't happen to see all of those white people in the crowd who were happy about the outcome? Somebody had to win, so get over it."

He was shocked and I was disgusted, so I excused myself.

I do not respect anyone who could be classified as fanatical or who wants to argue with you over your decisions and feels the need to share their beliefs and why they are right and you are wrong. I respect the fact that people can choose what sex partner they prefer to date. I respect the fact that there are different types of religions for us to choose from, and I respect and absorb different cultures and ethnicities. While I have had the pleasure of going off on a few of our pilots, for the most part, they truly are great guys and I really do appreciate the ones that take care of their flight crews and care about our safety.

Ending your shift with a cocktail or two in an unfamiliar city can sometimes even put us in dangerous situations that we may or may not live to regret.

Last month, I was flying to New York with a crew I really liked. Because I liked them, I agreed to meet them in the bar for a drink despite the fact that it was already nearing 1:00 AM. My crew and I sat at a table across from another table containing three flight attendants we did not know. I could tell by their attire of cheap, tacky, skintight clothes, with their boobs hanging out, and their loud mouths, that they were looking for some action or at least for some free drinks. About thirty minutes into our drinks, a security guard came to usher everyone out because it was last call. I heard one of the tacky flight attendants loudly ask the bartender if there was another bar nearby because she wanted to par-tay. A guy I'd noticed sitting at the bar checking out their table all night chimed in (probably hoping to be invited) that he knew of a place. They started talking and despite protests from her crewmembers, she left with him. The next day, she failed to make her lobby time and didn't answer the phone in her room or her cell phone. Security went to her room and found her bloody and beaten up with a concussion. I found out later that the dude from the bar had put a date-rape drug in her drink and taken advantage of her. I felt sorry for her, but I still found it hard to believe that, at her age, and after all of the literature my company distributes about safety, she still chose to leave her friends to go out with a complete stranger in an unfamiliar city.

Situations like this remind me why I choose to keep to myself, keep a low profile, and use my common sense and good judgment.

Flight attendants do have stalkers and are subjected to predators who seek us out, but it is rare we encounter such extreme behavior; however, it is not rare to encounter the occasional douche bag.

DOUCHE BAGS

Flight attendants get hit on all of the time and some men have no shame. I cannot tell you how many times I have been hit on by married men. I guess it is a fantasy of theirs to be able to jet set around the world for business meetings and have a "girlfriend" that can easily hop on a flight to meet them for the night or for the weekend. While some people do engage in that type of behavior, I do not and I get highly offended when someone suggests that I start. So offended, that I might just tell your wife.

One time, I was accosted by a guy on my flight and, after constant urging from the other flight attendants, I gave him my number. Let me make this clear—in all of the years that I have been flying, I have only given my number out to men three times. I am at work and it just feels weird and uncomfortable to fraternize with the customers. Anyway, Mark was so gorgeous, that he made me nervous just talking to him. So nervous that by the end of the flight, I had noticeable sweat stains under my arms.

After we met, Mark and I communicated every day. He wanted me to fly to Phoenix to hang out. Before I agreed, I did a Google search on Mark. I found out he did not have a Facebook page or any type of social media profile, which was kind of weird. Also, some of the things he told me (like the fact that he played football for a big ten school) didn't yield any results on the internet either. He was very secretive about his career and because he said he was ex military, I thought he was part of the CIA or something. Mark claimed he was recently divorced and he made the mistake of telling me too many details about his "ex" wife.

About a week after our encounter, I knew things weren't adding up. I began digging further on the internet and bingo, I found a YouTube video of his proposal to his "ex" wife. Through posted comments, I was able to find a link to the videographer's home page that included a two-minute video of their wedding. After further probing, I hit the jackpot! I discovered a link to his "ex" wife's Facebook profile! I thought it was odd that she still had a picture from their wedding day as her profile photo if they were divorced. Remembering that he told me she was a doctor, I was able to do a quick Google search of her name and profession and I called her. She was shocked, but because of me she found out her husband had an email address that she was not aware of and a texting app he was using to communicate with me and about eight other women. After showing her his selfies and "particular" photos of himself he had sent me, I made sure there was no way he could get out of his sticky situation. I felt sorry for his wife because she'd had bad feelings for a while that something was up. While she thanked me for doing the right thing, he was pissed and sent me a text saying he hoped my plane would crash!

SOCIAL MEDIA

In the age of "please, please look at me and how awesome I think I am", we have a bevy of social media avenues at our disposal—Facebook, Twitter, LinkedIn, Google+ and Instagram, just to name a few (by the way, check out my social media profiles . . . hahaha). I have a love/hate relationship with social media. I love to stay current with the news, but I get tired of tuning in to CNN and hearing the same stories over and over again as if they have nothing else to report about. Social media has an impressive reach and will keep you posted on everything happening around the world, not just a select few stories. I also love that I can log on and see what a friend has been up to and I can view current photos.

What I hate about social media is the constant selfies! Enough already! I wish there was a selfie limit. I am sure I am not alone with these thoughts.

I get tired of seeing flight attendant selfies all done the same way—inside of an overhead bin, sitting on the jumpseat, or sitting inside of an engine. Can we please get some originality around here? We have some crazy-ass flight attendants who love to post "TMI" on social media sites, specifically Facebook and Instagram. While it is certainly appropriate for you to use social media, my company frowns on people who post inappropriate comments and photos. Knowing that the company can and will look at our social media sites, some flight attendants still post pictures of themselves posing with their nightly cocktails. We have one brunette bimbo who is known for posting her tacky selfies, wearing bikinis and cheap stripper heels while consuming her "dinner" of wine mixed with a cocktail of Xanax and Hydrocodone before having to report for work the next morning. The things people will do for attention.

I get a kick out of the ones that call in sick for work and then post pictures of themselves getting trashed on the beach or celebrating their kid's birthday. Word of advice: if you don't want to get fired, remove the date and time stamp from your photos.

When you are off the company clock, you are free to do what you want, do who you want, and discuss whatever tickles your fancy. What tickles my fancy is this . . .

To my fellow flight attendants:

STOP stealing from your fellow employees! In the words of Britney Spears, "You betta work, Bitch!" If I catch you going in my purse, it will be the last purse you will ever steal from.

STOP looking like a hot mess in your ill-fitting uniform. I know when you left the house that you did not see anything wrong with your appearance. Now that you are standing next to me, you have a million excuses for why you look like shit. Do you know what a tailor is? A tailor is someone who measures your body and sews your clothes to fit you perfectly. See what a little bit of effort can do for you? Now, you don't have to continue to stand next to me and feel like chopped liver. You should come to work looking as if you are going to an audition for a movie. You never know who you might run into. I am sick and tired of seeing ungroomed flight attendants. You piss me off when you always want to keep the cabin dark to enhance your beauty. You wouldn't need the cabin so dark if you took a few minutes to comb your hair, tuck in your shirt, and maybe put on a girdle and some make-up. Be respectful and remember that I am dark and when it's dark in here, the passengers cannot see me.

STOP getting on the hotel shuttle and rudely interrupting me while I am on my phone because you need some attention. You have the nerve to call me rude, but you're the one who got in my face, violating my personal space. I like how you had the nerve to say you're tired of rude people and, when I call your ass out loudly in front of everyone, asking you if you were talking to me, you reply with, "No, I am talking in general." Yeah, that's what I thought.

AND ANOTHER THING THAT GETS ON MY NERVES . . .

If you want to commit suicide, go ahead, just do it at home on your own damned time! Thanks to the last person who pulled this move, I was stuck at some dump near the airport with a subpar workout room when we were kicked out of my favorite, 5-Star hotel in the heart of downtown. Thanks for being so selfish!

Chapter 18

Dear Diary,

What happens in the cockpit stays in the cockpit.

There are two types of cockpits, the cockpit on the plane, and the cockpit in the hotel room. Before we delve into either "cock" pit, let me describe a typical pilot for you.

A typical pilot is a white man who usually earned his flight hours by joining the Air Force. They were usually the geek in school who was picked on and vowed one day that everyone would eat his shit. Now he is all grown up, has developed a God-like complex, and struts around as if he is the chosen one because he is being highly paid to get you safely from point A to point B. Even if you don't notice the stripes on their shoulders, you can probably tell this man is the captain. But having money doesn't mean a thing if you have no class and no style.

Captains make a lot of money but don't be fooled; they are notoriously cheap and most just don't give a damn about their appearance. When you see a pilot walking around with their pants too short, prompting you to inquire, "Dude, where's the flood?" he's most likely the first officer. While they do not make the same salary as the captain, they still do very well for themselves, so the short pants are a mystery to me.

I rarely see a well-groomed pilot, but when I do, I always make it a point to compliment them. Even if he is an ass, at least he took the time to put some effort into his appearance. Some pilots strut around with Dunlap's disease (your gut "done lapped" over your waistline). Regardless of attire or appearance, the majority of pilots are boring Republicans (or pretend to be), who live in the suburbs with a wife (usually wife #2, i.e., the upgraded wife to go with the upgrade to the left seat). They usually have at least two kids and own either a boat or a Cessna. A lot of them are very homophobic (or pretend to be). Yeah, sounds pretty lame and cookie cutter to me too, but don't let the description fool you. While maybe 5% are totally faithful, upstanding guys, a vast majority of pilots get down and dirty when the epaulets come off. Athletes are not the only ones with groupies. Pilots have them too. There is a small group of flight attendants whose only ambition is to nail a pilot. They don't care if he is married. The goal is the paycheck and the way to achieve the paycheck is to get pregnant and hope that a child will eventually lead to marriage. These dogged women want only to stay at home and be "kept". That's a pathetic goal to have, and when you find out he is having an affair, I will not feel sorry for you. You are just like the wives of athletes who knew what they were getting themselves into. Just because he married you doesn't mean that he's changed. You just happened to catch him at a vulnerable moment, and like most guys, he was just too lazy and too stupid to know better.

Back in the day, if you were a new flight attendant, you had to go through a rite of passage and flash your boobs in the cockpit. I would never reduce my character to such lows and my boobs are so little that I don't even excite myself.

Now, these sluts are taking it to a "whole nutha level" (thanks *MADtv*), by performing fellatio and having sex in the cockpit! Are you wondering where the other pilot is? Oh, he's watching and hoping he's next or he's in the cabin taking a long bathroom break. I have suspected some of this type of behavior in the past, but I couldn't prove it (though the participant's shifty eyes gave them away).

Some flight attendants make their move in the bar by being overly sympathetic while listening to the pilot's stories about the wife they will not leave because they are afraid they will have to give her half of their money. It's cheaper to keep her and so they opt to have affairs on the side. Some affairs are short lived, as in one-night stands, while others turn into romances that last for years.

Have you ever read *The Pilot's Wife* by Anita Shreve? If not, I strongly suggest that, if you are married to or planning on getting married to a pilot, you read her book the first chance you get. What happens in the book is very true and it happens a lot more than you think. I will admit, having an entire family in another country is rare. They usually like to keep them closer to home.

I am not going to put the blame entirely on the female flight attendants because pilots always have a game plan.

Don't let the t-shirt with the holes in it, the old, ripped, non-stylish jeans, and moccasins with no socks, fool you. Pilots have plenty of game!

We had a pilot in his 60's who had to retire because of age limitations. He couldn't imagine giving up his mistress and staying at home with his wife every day, so for three months he dressed in his uniform and packed his bag as if he was going to work for a three or four day trip. He would come home from work and tell his wife all about his travels. One day, she had an emergency and could not get hold of him on his cell phone because it was turned off (because he was "flying"). His wife called the pilot and crew-scheduling department only to be told that her husband had retired months before! I am sure when he got home that week from his "trip" that all hell broke loose.

About ten years ago, I was flying with a girl named Mary who had a reputation for getting her knees dirty, if you know what I mean. She had a drinking habit and everybody knew it (remember The List?). I felt sorry for her because she was a single mother in her late thirties with a teenage son. It was obvious she just wanted somebody to love her, but guys just kept taking advantage of her. She did not do herself any favors by wearing skin tight t-shirts to show off her boobs and daisy duke shorts. Once, a bunch of us were sitting at a bar when the pilot we had flown with that day sidled up next to Mary and offered to buy our drinks. I remembered he had been wearing a wedding ring when we were flying, but that night it was gone. Mary started flirting with him, believing he was single and, as the drinks kept coming, Mary grew looser by the second. After my third drink, I couldn't take the shit show anymore and I left her at the bar.

The next morning, Mary showed up late for our lobby pick up because she had a hangover. She stank of beer and sex, so of course, I knew what had gone down, and I wanted the scoop. She told me that, shortly after I'd left her, she had downed her sixth drink and then headed with the pilot to his room. After fifteen minutes, it was over and she stumbled back to her room. He promised to call her (which I am sure he never did because she said he hadn't asked for her phone number). I saw that same pilot the following week and he was as cool as a cucumber. I am sure he knew that I knew about his dirty deeds, just as I am sure he knew that I was aware that he was married with kids after I made a point to ask about them. I am also sure this was not his first, nor would it be his last time dabbling in raunchy affairs on an overnight.

Years ago, when I was based in Texas, I was flying with two flight attendants named Heather and Rachel. While pouring drinks in the back galley, I learned that they were talking about their relationship problems. Apparently, both women were dating a pilot whom they each suspected of cheating. I just took it all in because I love good gossip. By the third flight, I was zoned out reading my book on the back jumpseat, when I heard multiple passenger call buttons going off. I was alarmed and thought we must have a serious emergency on our hands. As I made my way into the cabin, all I could gather was that somebody was fighting. When I managed to get the lookie loos aside, I was shocked to see that Heather and Rachel were the two fighting! Names were being called, punches and slaps passed between them, and hair extensions and heels went flying. We had to make an emergency landing due to the incident. They were both removed from the flight and hauled off to jail. I found out later that while they were doing the usual jumpseat confession, they realized they were both dating the same damned pilot! What made it even fouler was that Heather and Rachel were located at the same base.

Listen up pilots . . . if you are going to do dirty things (which so many of you do) keep it clean and don't dabble in the same base. Idiots!

CULTURE-LESS

We all know that a majority of pilots belong to the "good old boys club". For that reason, you rarely come across a pilot with any culture.

As I mentioned earlier, pilots are usually very cookie cutter and so are their wives. She is usually a stay-at-home mom who is either blonde or brunette with big boobs. It is rare to see a pilot with a woman of color. Hell, even a ginger would be nice from time to time.

I know some of them are afraid to rock the boat, and I think it's silly when they look at me wistfully and wish I was theirs. I can tell the difference between the ones that really have flavor and the ones who are just curious. The ones that have flavor have a certain je ne sais quoi to them that is obvious in their walk and their demeanor. They don't have to pretend that they are cool because they are and it shows. I can tell by the demeanor of the rest of the geeks that they would not know the first thing about dating someone outside their own race.

I don't care to hear stories specifically about the black celebrities they saw on TV and I don't want to hear about anyone's black friend. I will let you in on a secret . . . someone who is cultured would say, "I have a beautiful girlfriend."

Someone who is not cultured would say, "I have a beautiful black girlfriend."

See the difference?

I'll allow some of them to stand in my galley and flirt with me because I know this is the highlight of their days, but while I tolerate their goofiness, I am rolling my eyes inside because I know that if I gave them more than the time of day they would not know how to explain it to their families.

The other day, as I was getting off my flight, the new pilots were coming onboard. As I was gathering my belongings, one of them stood there staring at me a beat too long and couldn't stop himself from going there.

"Oh my God, you look like Nikki Minaj!" he said.

"Excuse me? Nikki Minaj! Do you know she has an ass the size of a dump truck?"

"No, I didn't know that."

"I usually get Naomi Campbell or Kerry Washington, but never Nikki Minaj. Outside of our hairstyle, we look nothing alike."

"I'm sorry. I was just saying I think you are pretty."

No, what he was saying was that he thought all black

people look alike when it would have been better for him to just stand there and be quiet. Furthermore, he just proved he really didn't know who in the hell Nikki Minaj is because she is most famous for her "assets" and everybody knows this. As I deplaned, he had the nerve to say, "Bye, Nikki!"

Jackass!

So, pilots? Stop trying so hard to be cool because it is not becoming and you are just embarrassing yourselves.

Do I Look Like a Maid?

The thing that chaps my hide more than making hot chocolate is when pilots act as if they are helpless and that I am the paid help. We offer them snacks and beverages because it is a nice thing to do and doesn't ruin our days. Some of you get onboard, get your luggage stowed, stand in my galley shooting the breeze, climb into the cockpit to make your checks and then holler at me to get you something to drink. Weren't you just standing here? The last time I checked, your hands were working properly or else you would not be flying this jet. Don't give me that lame-ass excuse that you don't know where anything is, because I will gladly show you where the ice and drinks are so you can help yourself. And while I am giving you a tour of my galley, let me show you where the trashcan is located.

Pilots always keep a trash bag in the cockpit for the trash they collect throughout the day. At the end of the day, they are supposed to dispose of their bag in the trashcan, but too many of them just throw it on the floor of my galley as if they have a maid on the aircraft. I understand that you do not have any authority when you are at home, and that you love to come to work and assert yourself, but if you continue to throw your trash on the floor as if you do not have any manners, I am going to call you out on it and I don't care if you are not happy.

I'M NOT GAY

I am going to do you pilots a favor and provide you with the definition of "gay", and I am not talking about being gay as in being happy either. According to the Merriam-Webster Dictionary, gay means to be sexually attracted to someone who is the same sex. Here are some examples in case you are still confused: a man sleeping with another man = GAY. Allowing another man to go down on you whether you reciprocate or not = GAY. You do understand that allowing my precious members of the Rainbow Coalition to suck your weenie makes you GAY, right? No? You still don't think you are GAY? Well, then try sharing your encounters with your friends. Hell, even try your wife on for a size and see if she doesn't divorce your ass in a New York minute. Hint: if I were you, I would just say you were inquiring for a friend.

There are very few pilots who have the balls to admit they are openly gay and I applaud the ones who do and respect them tremendously. I know that people who are "out" run the risk of being isolated, teased, and possibly treated unfairly by people who envy them for being able to be themselves—open and proud without living the life of a liar, fearing rejection from loved ones.

Most pilots are Republicans and supposedly anti-gay, until you get their ass to the bar on an overnight and they become a little too comfortable with a male flight attendant.

I am the President of the Rainbow Coalition and I love gay men. Some act more feminine than I do and I am the real thing. I do not trust gay men like that because they are usually too loud, overly aggressive, and prone to exaggeration and lying. The gay guys I adore are regal, tactful, and quiet men who understand that they can let the world know that they are gay without being overt in their mannerisms. My boys are comfortable with who they are. They are proud and they don't lie.

Once, I was working a trip with my friends Paul and Mark. Paul was gay and Mark was straight. After introducing ourselves to the pilots, we went to our respective boarding positions on the aircraft.

When Ryan, our captain, saw that I was the lead flight attendant, he said he was relieved and said he'd had all male crews for the past two weeks in a row and was just happy to see my pretty face. Of course, he prefaced this by saying, "I hope this doesn't offend you."

You can be assured that when somebody prefaces a conversation with this phrase, it is always going to be something offensive. You all know by now that I am not easily offended, so his comment was no big deal. I had heard it many times before.

I would feel the same if I was constantly being bombarded by lesbians. We flew the entire day and ended up on an overnight together. By the time we arrived at the hotel, it was already late, so we agreed to meet in the bar for food and drinks. It is always a little disconcerting at first, to see your fellow crewmembers in street clothes because we always look very different outside of the uniform. Ryan had just commented on how different I looked when Paul walked into the bar looking like a model. Paul just oozed class and he carried himself in a very confident way. He looked so great that even Ryan felt the need to confirm the obvious. When we all sat down, Ryan sat by Paul, which at the time seemed like no big deal. I did not think anything of it, but Paul got this look in his eye like he was trying to convey a message to me that I failed to understand. I was clueless, but not so clueless that I didn't notice that within the hour, and after several glasses of wine, Ryan got really comfortable and a little touchy-feely with Paul. It was subtle, but my gaydar was up and running and I smelled something fishy. We all left the bar about two hours later. On our way back to the elevator, Ryan stopped at the front desk and asked to see the pilot and flight attendant sign-in sheets. A sign-in sheet is a form that we fill out upon checking into every hotel. It lists your base, your employee number, your name, and your room number. In a nutshell, employees can and do stalk each other. Kind of creepy. We always check the list to see if we recognize a friend's name on the list. I did not think anything about Ryan wanting to see the list, and went ahead of him to my room.

The next day at our lobby pick up, we were not flying with the same pilots, so I asked Paul about the signals he tried to send me the night before at the bar. The story he shared left me speechless. Apparently, when Ryan asked for the sign-in sheet, he requested to see the flight attendant's sheet and he got Paul's room number.

Paul was in his room getting ready for bed when the phone in his room rang. "Hello?" he said, knowing exactly who it was.

"Hey, Paul. This is Ryan. I was wondering if you could come over and give me some advice on a couple of things."

Paul stalled. "Advice?"

Ryan chuckled nervously. "Yeah, I just really need your help with some fashion advice."

Paul, of course, knew what that meant and was more than happy to help Ryan with his "dilemma". When he knocked on Ryan's door, he noticed that Ryan had the security latch holding the door ajar.

"Thanks for coming by. I just want you to know that I'm not gay, but I just think you are a really sharp dude," Ryan said.

"No worries, your secret is safe with me."

It is safe, for now, until you piss me off and get on my bad side. I know you do not remember who I am, but I know who you are and if you make a single homophobic comment in my presence, I will make you eat your words.

In the previous chapter, I told you the story of a resident on Shutter Island named Nancy. You remember the one who randomly pulled her boobs out while making drinks for passengers? Yeah, that one. Nancy was married to one of our pilots. Things seemed to be going well until, after a few years into the marriage, he just started acting weird. He barely touched her at night. He started picking up extra flights despite the fact that they were financially sound, and he began accusing her of having an affair (ladies, I think we all know what that means). His accusations made her suspicious because she was not having an affair, but she soon suspected he was. She confronted him and he denied having an affair. To squash her feelings, he bought her flowers, took her shopping, and they went on a weeklong vacation to Hawaii. When they returned from their trip, Nancy was on cloud nine and had never felt better. About a week later, her husband went to work and had an overnight in Los Angeles. Wanting to keep the high of euphoria, Nancy decided that she would surprise her husband on his overnight. When Nancy got to the hotel, she flashed her airline ID, checked the sign-in sheet, and then asked for a key to her husband's room. When she got to his room, she listened at the door for a few minutes to check to see if he was there, but she wasn't prepared for what had to have been the shock of her life. She heard two male voices and the sounds of making out. Heart racing, Nancy swiped the key, but when she went to open his door, she found the security latch was in place preventing her from going any further. She still caught sight of the men jumping up from the bed. Nancy went wild and starting screaming, cussing, and trying to kick in the door. Security and the police were called to remedy the situation. After this incident, she started having psychotic episodes that only seemed to occur when she was flying with men.

I know some of you may find this quite shocking. It was to me when I caught wind of the dirty deeds that go on in the "cock" pit too. But hey, pilots are no different than politicians with their fancy footwork or catholic priests hiding their erections behind their robes in the name of Jesus. Pilots are just like the men who sit across from your cubicle, the ones who always seem to be with all of these women nobody ever sees. They are married to your sister who emphatically denies her husband is gay despite the fact that everybody swears something is just not right. He is your dentist, who just performed "oral" surgery on your little brother. The point is this—if you are not offended by this chapter, you have nothing to hide. The ones who are offended . . . come out, come out, wherever you are.

Chapter 19

Before I go.

LMFAO (laughing my f-ing ass off)

I know the title of this book is Diary of a Pissed-Off Flight Attendant. While I get pissed off from time to time, you guys make my day by making me feel special and pretty or just by making me laugh so hard, I pee my pants.

Just this past December, I had a sour moment at work (what's new, right?).

I went to ask this gentleman for his drink order. "Sir, can I get you anything to drink?"

"Yes, can I have a can of Coke and a date?" He smiled.

He was so slick that he left me blushing and speechless. That line was so cute that if I didn't already have a boyfriend, and Henry hadn't been a tad too chubby for my taste, I would have so given him my number.

Due to the crazy weather this past December, we canceled tons of flights. Passengers were camped out in the airport as if they were in a refugee camp. Everybody—airline personnel, the airport vendors, even the pets—was pissed off. As my crew and I were walking to our plane, (of course our flight wasn't canceled!) we overheard an exchange between a gate agent and a passenger.

"Sir, I understand your frustration, but hollering at me is not going to help your situation," the agent said.

"You don't understand shit!! And it seems to me that talking to you isn't getting me anywhere either, you stupid bitch!" the passenger spit.

"Sir, I am calling the authorities."

The passenger reached over the desk, grabbed the agent's computer keyboard, and conked him on the head with it. "Now you have a reason to call the damned authorities!"

OH. MY. GOD. My stomach hurt so badly from laughing that I got cramps. I should have checked to see if the agent was all right, but I did not want to be next.

Every day is an adventure and just when you think you have seen or heard it all, somebody always comes along and surprises you. I would not trade my career for anything (except, of course, if I won the lottery). No other job offers the flexibility or the downtime that my job offers. I have so much downtime at work that I wrote this entire book while on the plane, in between serving customers. It is awesome that when I wake up tomorrow, if I do not want to be gone for three days, that I can switch my trip to a one day trip. We make a very nice salary and I know that I make more money than many of my friends with Master's Degrees. We do not have to take our jobs home with us other than to tell crazy stories and we do not have to work eighty-hour weeks (unless we want to) to make an incredible living. I know, it's not fair, but somebody has to do it, so it might as well be me. What other job out there allows you to work with different people every time you go to work? No other job gives you the option to jet set all over the world, visiting friends and family on the company's dime, reminding us that we do live the "Glamorous Life" (thanks, Fergie).

We are away from our families for days at a time and sometimes it can be tough. There is nothing worse than being on an overnight and getting an emergency phone call in the middle of the night because, chances are, you cannot do anything about it except wait until the morning when you can hop on the next flight home.

So the next time I snobbishly cut you off at security and you call me a bitch under your breath, remember this. . . I am that same bitch who will perform the Heimlich maneuver on you when you are choking on a chili cheese dog (or maybe not; you shouldn't be eating that crap anyway). I am also the same bitch who will save your ass in the event of an emergency evacuation. Never mind the fact that I am already safely off the plane and on the ground, yelling at you to cover your nose and mouth, get below the smoke, and follow the light.

I want to leave you with this: I am NOT a bitch . . . I am nicely rude.

Thank You

First, I want to thank you, the passengers, for your endless ignorance and antics. Without you, I would not have a job, nor would I have been capable of writing this book.

My beautiful aunt, MC, for raising me, encouraging me, and for always cheering me on and being proud of me. Thank you for always reminding me to "say my prayers"!

My beloved and biggest supporter, JC, for being my rock. I love you, Honey!

My parents, TS and JS, for all you have done for me.

My two surrogate families, MT/DT and FH/MH, for allowing me to be a part of your loving families. I would not have survived if not for your help, support, and love.

My BFF, VR, who encouraged me years ago to write this book. Thank you for your wisdom and guidance for twenty-one years.

My BFF, SH, for always having my back and laughingly always calling me a "stupid ass".

I will always love you KG for taking me in when times were rough. You have been by my side since I was a young adult and I will always cherish your friendship.

My dear friend, LF, for your courage, your unrelenting spirit, your positive energy and for showing me that God is always near.

My beautiful sister, TS, for knowing I'm a "bit much"

and loving me anyway.

My amazing and beautiful aunt, PW, for always being glamorous and fashionable and giving me someone to emulate.

My favorite cousin in the world, RE, for being the most loyal and loving cousin that ever lived.

Thanks to SR for renewing my energy to complete this book.

A ton of thanks to GB for helping me with the title and for showing me, a complete stranger at the time, an amazing time in your country.

A special thank you to LL for taking me under your wing. God works in mysterious ways, and I will be forever grateful for our chance encounter.

My beautiful and talented big sister, TH, for always being there for me. Without you, I would not have my career. I will always love you for encouraging me to stay at Sun Airways.

A big thank you and many hugs to my amazing team of editors, Ken and Michele at Full Sail Editing. I could not have done this without your help and knowledge. Thank you for holding my hand and being patient with me.

Thank you to my kick ass team at Smith Publicity.

Lots of hugs and kisses and many thanks to the entire Stark Team for letting me stress you out with constant deadlines. You guys rock!

You're my boy, B. Nix! Thanks for the endless legal explanations and for all of the time and effort you put into helping me with this book and my business endeavors.

Finally, I want to thank all of my fellow flight attendants for their hard work, dedication, and the bitch-fests.

About the Author

Sydney Pearl is a freelance writer and author of *Diary of a Pissed-Off Flight Attendant*. She became an avid reader at the age of five to help raise money for her aunt to participate in the Special Olympics. Her love of books continued, inspiring her to write her first book. Sydney is an active flight attendant for a well-respected airline. She is in a beautiful relationship and lives in Chicago, Illinois.

Website: www.diaryofapissedoffflightattendant.com
Twitter: @sydneypearl747
Google+: sydneypearl747@gmail.com
Facebook Page: Diary of a Pissed Off Flight Attendant